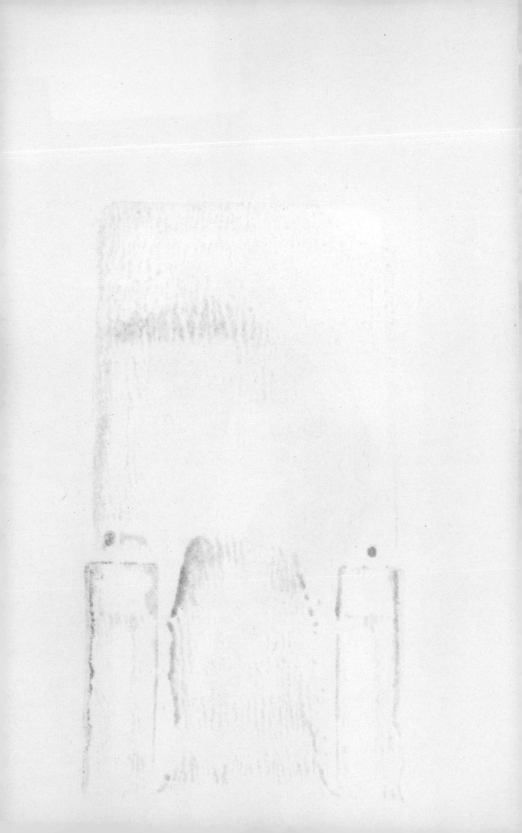

OXFORD ENGLISH MONOGRAPHS

General Editors

ALICE WALKER   NORMAN DAVIS
HELEN GARDNER

OXFORD ENGLISH MONOGRAPHS

Chapter 11.

Who can ~~sweat anything~~ Who can be in doubt of what followed? When any two young People take it into their heads to marry, they are pretty sure by perseverance to ~~carry their point~~ ~~the op position~~ be they ever so poor, or ever so imprudent, or ever so little likely to be necessary to each other's ultimate comfort. This may be bad Morality to conclude with, but I believe it to be Truth — and if such practices succeed, how should Capt W. & an. Anne fail, with the advantage of maturity of Mind, consciousness of Right, & ~~my~~ one independant Fortune between ~~them~~, of bearing down every opposition? They might in fact, have borne down a great deal more than they met with, for there was little to distress them beyond the want of Graciousness & Warmth. Sir W. made no objection, & Eliz: did nothing worse than look cold & unconcerned. — Capt W. with £25,000 — & as high in his

The first page of the manuscript Chapter 11 of *Persuasion*
(three-quarters full size)
British Museum Egerton MS. 3038

JANE AUSTEN'S LITERARY MANUSCRIPTS

*A study of the
novelist's development through
the surviving papers*

BY

B. C. SOUTHAM

OXFORD UNIVERSITY PRESS

1964

Oxford University Press, Amen House, London E.C.4

GLASGOW NEW YORK TORONTO MELBOURNE WELLINGTON
BOMBAY CALCUTTA MADRAS KARACHI LAHORE DACCA
CAPE TOWN SALISBURY NAIROBI IBADAN ACCRA
KUALA LUMPUR HONG KONG

© *Oxford University Press 1964*

PRINTED IN GREAT BRITAIN

PREFACE

MY purpose in this study has been to examine the surviving literary manuscripts of Jane Austen in order to establish the course of her writing outside the major works and to relate this to her development in the six novels. The manuscript works reveal every stage in the formation of the novelist's art, from the burlesque trifles and entertainment pieces of her childhood to the writing of her full maturity, a progress extending over thirty years, from about 1787 to 1817.

The earliest pieces are found in the three notebooks, *Volume the First*, *Volume the Second*, and *Volume the Third*. These contain transcripts of the juvenilia, composed between about 1787 (when she was twelve) and 1793. In 1793 or 1794 she wrote *Lady Susan*, which survives in a fair copy made some years later. Between 1795 and 1799 Jane Austen was at work upon the early versions of *Sense and Sensibility*, *Pride and Prejudice* and *Northanger Abbey*, but of these no manuscript remains. A fourth novel, *The Watsons*, was begun in 1804, and we have the uncompleted first draft. Of the three later novels—*Mansfield Park*, *Emma*, and *Persuasion*—written between 1811 and 1816, there survives a single manuscript fragment, the original ending to *Persuasion*, two chapters written in July 1816. To the same period belongs a fair copy of the burlesque *Plan of a Novel*. Finally, and most important, we have the unfinished first draft of *Sanditon*, Jane Austen's last work, abandoned in March 1817, three months before her death.

My discussion of the manuscript material touches upon a number of biographical and textual questions: the influence of Jane Austen's family and her childhood reading upon her work; the chronology of composition; and the details of correction and revision of the manuscripts provide our clearest view of the artist at work. However, the manuscript material is of greatest value for what it reveals of Jane Austen's development. All too often this has been regarded as a self-contained and final process, beginning in *Sense and Sensibility* and culminating in *Persuasion*. The manuscripts encourage us to take a somewhat different view. We see that the six novels stand at the end of a long apprenticeship. The 'little touches of human truth, little glimpses of steady vision, little master-strokes of imagination' were not, as Henry James fancied, the issue of 'the extraordinary grace of her facility ... of her unconsciousness'.[1] They were the rewards of laborious composition, of trial and error, the art of the novelist won through many years of highly conscious experiment. And in *Sanditon* the mature artist sought to extend her range even further, in directions scarcely hinted at in the earlier novels. She strove to evolve a more complex and refined narrative method, to explore figurative and symbolic devices in language and action, to form an expressive style, and to communicate a new and strangely mixed feeling, a sense both of delight and disillusionment with man and the comedy of his existence. In *Sense and Sensibility* Jane Austen declares herself a daughter of Dr. Johnson; in *Sanditon* we recognize a writer of the nineteenth century, with her own 'lawful issue' (as Kipling's messwaiter remarks) in the works of ' 'Enery James'.

Only recently has it been possible to follow this development in its entirety. The manuscripts have been difficult of access, and their publication delayed and spread over a number of years. All the substantial works, except the juvenilia, were first printed or referred to as early as 1871, in the second edition of the *Memoir*. But the record there was neither accurate nor complete: *Lady Susan* was printed from a copy of the manuscript, the original having been mislaid; the *Plan of a Novel* was silently altered and reduced; one of the two chapters of *Persuasion* was omitted; and the extracts from *Sanditon* amounted to only one-sixth of the total work. Full and definitive texts gradually became available in Dr. Chapman's separate editions, with their valuable introductions and textual notes, yet this series was not com-

---

[1] 'The Lesson of Balzac' (1905), in *The House of Fiction* (1957), ed. Leon Edel, p. 63.

pleted until the appearance of *Volume the Third* in 1951; and until the edition of *Volume the Second* in 1963 the details of correction and revision in that notebook were unknown. Thus to a great extent the previous discussion of these works has been hampered by lack of knowledge. Moreover, there has been a tendency among critics either to study the pieces in isolation (an unsuitable approach for works which are fragmentary or closely related to other writing), or, at the other extreme, to argue speculatively that there is a direct and visible relationship between Jane Austen's life and art, and between the early and later writing. The leading proponent of this theory is Mrs. Q. D. Leavis, who maintains that the juvenilia, *Lady Susan* and *The Watsons* are the quarry for at least two of the novels; and that details of the action and characterization in *Lady Susan* and *Mansfield Park* are partly derived from events and persons in the Austen household.[1] As this important and influential theory is still current, and likely to gain further circulation by the reprinting of *Scrutiny*, I have examined its basic assumptions and methods in the Appendix. Amongst all the writings about Jane Austen, I have found the most instructive and stimulating criticism in the works of Miss Mary Lascelles and Professor Marvin Mudrick, whose prime concern has been with the novels.

In the preparation of this study my first debt is to Dr. Chapman, without whose editions our approach to Jane Austen would still be very uncertain. I would like to thank Mrs. Rosemary Mowll for her kindness in allowing me to examine the manuscript of *Volume the Second*; the Librarian of King's College, Cambridge, for access to the manuscript of *Sanditon*; Bodley's Librarian, for access to the manuscript of *Volume the First* and to Dr. Chapman's photostat facsimile of *Volume the Third*; the Keeper of Manuscripts, the British Museum, for access to the manuscript chapters of *Persuasion*; the Curator, Autograph Manuscripts, the Pierpont Morgan Library, for information and microfilms of *Lady Susan* and part of *The*

[1] *Scrutiny* (1941-2, 1944); cited in the Appendix, note 2, p. 136.

Watsons; and the Regents of the University of California, by whose permission material has been taken from an article that originally appeared in *Nineteenth Century Fiction*.

For their kind advice I am grateful to a number of friends, in particular to Mr. John Naylor, Professor Walton Litz of Princeton, and Mr. T. Edward Carpenter, Chairman of the Jane Austen Memorial Trust, who allowed me to examine his collection of manuscripts and has given me the benefit of his unrivalled knowledge of the Austen family. Mrs. Elsie Duncan-Jones and Dr. Ian Jack made a number of helpful comments when an earlier version of this study was presented as a thesis. My thanks also go to Mr. Roger Morkam for his careful reading and correction of my final typescript.

In conclusion, I am happy to acknowledge my greatest debt, to Miss Mary Lascelles, who originally drew my attention to the subject of this study and who has with considerable patience and generosity advised me throughout its preparation, although not necessarily agreeing with all its arguments and conclusions.

B. C. S.

Westfield College
University of London
March 1963

TABLE OF CONTENTS

REFERENCES

A list of works to which frequent reference is made

UNLESS otherwise stated, all references are to the editions of R. W. Chapman:

Volume the First, 1933.
Volume the Second, 1963, ed. B. C. Southam.
Volume the Third, 1951.
Lady Susan, 1925.
The Watsons, 1927.
Plan of a Novel, 1926.
Two Chapters of Persuasion, 1926.
Fragment of a Novel (Sanditon), 1925.
Minor Works, 1954.
Jane Austen's Letters, second edition, 1952.
The novels, in the Oxford Jane Austen, third edition, 1953.

The following forms of reference are employed for other works

Biographical Notice	Henry Austen, 'Biographical Notice of the Author', dated December 1817, prefaced to *Northanger Abbey* and *Persuasion*, 1818. (The 'Memoir of Miss Austen', dated October 1832, prefaced to Bentley's edition of *Sense and Sensibility*, 1833, is an altered version of the *Biographical Notice*.)
1870 *Memoir*	J. E. Austen-Leigh, *A Memoir of Jane Austen*, 1870.
1871 *Memoir*	Second edition, slightly changed, and including some of the manuscript material.
Hill	Constance Hill, *Jane Austen: Her Homes and her Friends*, 1902.
Life	W. and R. A. Austen-Leigh, *Jane Austen: Her Life and Letters*, 1913.
Personal Aspects	M. A. Austen-Leigh, *Personal Aspects of Jane Austen*, 1920.

REFERENCES

Jane Austen Mary Lascelles, *Jane Austen and Her Art*, 1939.

Austen Papers Ed. R. A. Austen-Leigh, *Austen Papers, 1704–1856*, 1942.

Facts and Problems R. W. Chapman, *Jane Austen: Facts and Problems*, 1948.

My Aunt Caroline Austen, *My Aunt Jane Austen*, 1952.

Critical Bibliography R. W. Chapman, *Jane Austen: A Critical Bibliography*, second edition, 1955.

LIST OF MANUSCRIPTS USED

Volume the First, Bodleian Library (MS. Don.e.7).

Volume the Second, Mrs. Rosemary Mowll.

Volume the Third, British Museum Library (Loan MS. 52) formerly held by the trustees of the estate of the late R. A. Austen-Leigh, was not available when this study was in preparation; at the time I worked from the photostat Dr. Chapman used in the preparation of the 1951 edition (Bodleian Library, MS. Facs.d.77).

The two chapters of *Persuasion,* British Museum Library (Egerton MS. 3038).

Sanditon, King's College Library, Cambridge (Safe).

The following manuscripts, in the Pierpont Morgan Library, New York, were studied from microfilms:

Lady Susan (MA 1226).

Plan of a Novel (MA 1034; also studied in the facsimile reproduced in Dr. Chapman's 1926 edition).

The Watsons (MA 1034; this is a fragment of the manuscript, the first six leaves, to p. 13 in Dr. Chapman's 1927 edition. The remainder of the manuscript is in the possession of the legatees of W. Austen-Leigh, and is not available for inspection).

1

THE WRITING OF THE JUVENILIA

(1)

WE have a full record of Jane Austen's earliest development, for the childhood works have come down to us virtually complete, showing every detail of her progress between about 1787 (she was twelve in December of that year) and 1793. The survival of this material is not a matter of chance. During a period of fifteen or twenty years Jane Austen collected some twenty-nine of these early pieces, amounting to over 90,000 words, to transcribe them into the three notebooks. Later, in her lifetime and after her death, these manuscripts were prized in the family for their associations and as entertainment for the children. As distinct from the published novels this early writing, intimate in design, much of it fragmentary or unfinished, was regarded by the Austens as her private work intended only for themselves. Thus for many years it was unknown beyond the family.

The earliest account of Jane Austen's life, the *Biographical Notice* of 1817 (expanded in 1832), makes no reference to the juvenilia. The first hint that any such writing existed was made in the 1870 *Memoir*, which mentions 'an old copy-book containing several tales, some of which seem to have been composed while she was quite a girl',[1] stories 'of a slight and flimsy texture'.[2] This description fits *Volume the First*, although there is no certain indication which of the notebooks J. E. Austen-Leigh had actually seen. He printed nothing from it, pleading that 'it would be as unfair to expose this preliminary process to the world, as it would be to display all that goes on behind the

---

[1] p. 59.   [2] pp. 59–60.

curtain of the theatre before it is drawn up'.[1] None the less, this scruple was soon overcome. The following year, in the second edition of the *Memoir*, he printed much of the later manuscript material, and included 'The Mystery', a little play from *Volume the First*. In point of fact Austen-Leigh had wanted to include some of the childhood pieces in the first edition, but this plan was opposed in the family. It may have been felt that Jane Austen's reputation would not be served by making public her immature works, particularly as these contained a lively strain of eighteenth-century humour offensive to Victorian taste.

Forty years later the information given in the 1871 *Memoir* (which spoke of 'copybooks extant'[2]) was enlarged upon very slightly in the *Life and Letters*, with a description of *Volume the Third* and some of the items in *Volume the First*. Beyond this nothing was known of the juvenilia until the notebooks were printed separately between 1922 and 1951.

Meanwhile, the focus of critical attention has remained on the novels, beside which the early works are relatively unimportant. Only 'Love and Friendship' and 'The History of England' can stand on their own. Other works in the collection are amusing but many of them are mere trifles, their humour dependent on the private jokes of a close family circle, and their prime importance is for the biographer and literary historian. They reveal Jane Austen's response to her reading, the influence of an intimate and sympathetic audience, and, most valuably for our purpose, they record the gradual change as the young writer began to turn from burlesque entertainment to experiment in the techniques of fiction.

Her development both at this time and later is remarkable for its consistency and continuity; and in outlook and method the novels are intimately related to the juvenilia. *Sanditon*, her last work, is deeply grounded in literary satire, an element of meaning and design that can be traced through the work of thirty years, sometimes dominant as a leading feature of the style and structure, or, as in *Mansfield Park* and *Persuasion*, a subdued and delicate suggestion underlying the social comedy.

[1] p. 62.   [2] p. 42.

The literary satire in the earliest of the juvenilia is burlesque of the most direct kind. The target is ridiculed by a mocking imitation, which emphasizes the weaknesses and conventions of the original by exaggeration, diminution, or rearrangement. It is in effect a form of aesthetic and moral criticism, exposing faults of style and absurdities in the subject-matter, and challenging the values and assumptions of the other writer. Even at its simplest this method of satire demands a shrewdness and skill unusual in childhood writing. Yet so swiftly and completely was Jane Austen master of its techniques that in 1790, at the age of fourteen, she could produce 'Love and Friendship', the most amusing and incisive of all eighteenth-century attacks upon sentimental fiction. Clearly this is the work of precocious genius, of a young writer in full command of her material, certain in her outlook and assured in her manner. But the phrase 'precocious genius', apt as it is, does nothing to explain why Jane Austen began by writing in this mode; nor does it explain how her accomplishment in burlesque was so quickly won, in contrast to her slow and painstaking progress between 1791 and 1793, the period during which she was gradually evolving her patterns of social comedy. There is much to impress us in the later juvenilia—swift and vivid portraiture, high comedy, shrewd wit, fluent, realistic dialogue—but nothing sustained, nothing to compare with 'Love and Friendship' or 'The History of England'.

Her immediate success in the earliest juvenilia can be explained very shortly. To a certain extent the strength of these pieces is derived from an already flourishing burlesque tradition. Her quick mastery of style and manner is partly the reward of clever imitation. Then, by 1792, after 'The History of England', Jane Austen came to recognize that the possibilities of this mode were largely explored, and that burlesque, however skilfully employed, was not a sufficient vehicle for her view of life. The growth of artistic vision demanded a corresponding growth in form and technique, with fresh problems to explore and overcome. These considerations help us to understand the precocious maturity of the earliest work and the weaknesses of the later juvenilia, a consequence of the change from selective copying to original experiment. Yet this account does nothing to explain why Jane Austen adopted burlesque as her earliest mode, and why the various modifications of literary satire were to play such a significant part in her mature writing. For an answer to these questions we have to consider the importance of the family environment and her reading, the two areas of experience most deeply drawn upon in her art.

(II)

In its creative faculty Jane Austen's imagination was not strongly inventive or fanciful, the qualities of mind so evident, for example, in the juvenilia of the Brontës. For Jane Austen the act of creation was to give form and meaning to her observation of life and literature, shaping and enriching this material in a process of analysis, reflection, and judgement. As a child of twelve she found the most convenient and tractable subject-matter in her reading. Her critical temper and keen sense of fun were quick to fasten upon the obvious absurdities of sentimental fiction, which reached the height of its popularity in the 1780's and 1790's. Romances and sentimental novels had been common targets for parody since the days of Richardson, and the Austens themselves practised this kind of literary joke. So what we can suppose to have been the natural response of a critical intelligence was encouraged by the example of her own family and their presence as ready audience.

As we learn from the *Memoir* and the *Life*, Steventon Rectory provided an unusual and stimulating home for the young writer. There was 'the flow of native wit, with all the fun and nonsense of a large and clever family',[1] a conversation 'rich in shrewd remarks, bright with playfulness and humour'.[2] Three of her five brothers—James, Henry, and Charles—were minor versifiers

---

[1] *Life*, p. 15, quoting Mrs. Lefroy.
[2] Hill, p. 83, quoting unidentified family manuscripts.

and essayists, their slight creative talent possibly taken from their mother, a woman reputed for her wit. It was said that even into old age she could produce an impromptu story or verse on demand.[1] Nothing is known of Mr. Austen as a writer, but he read widely and encouraged his daughter in her work. Closest of all, in temperament and ability, was her sister, Cassandra. In 1796, replying to one of her letters, Jane Austen addressed her as 'the finest comic writer of the present age',[2] playful flattery no doubt, for the only evidence of her wit is fifteen lines of verse,[3] and the letters to her sister have disappeared. But her sharp satirical miniatures to 'The History of England'[4] survive to show us that the sisters were well matched.

The family group was constantly changing and constantly supplied with news. First James, then Henry, went to Oxford, and the younger brothers, the naval officers Charles and Francis, would spend their leave at home. There were also pupils at the Rectory under Mr. Austen's tuition; and in the neighbourhood was a wide circle of relatives and friends, young and old, some of whom Jane Austen favoured with her stories.

The most remarkable visitor during Jane Austen's childhood was her 'very pleasure-loving' cousin, Eliza de Feuillide,[5] the wife of a French aristocrat. Her arrival at Steventon in 1787 was quickly followed by the revival of a little dramatic company, made up from the Austens and their neighbouring friends. The barn was converted into a small theatre for productions in the summer holidays; at Christmas plays were performed in the house. For

[1] Fanny Lefroy, *Temple Bar*, lxvii (1883), 272–3. A poem composed 8 November 1814 was printed in the *Times Literary Supplement*, 19 August 1955, p. 484 (Geoffrey Grigson, 'New Letters from Jane Austen's Home').

[2] *Letters*, p. 8.

[3] There is a four-page manuscript, wholly in Jane Austen's hand, which gives this poem together with one each by herself, Mrs. Austen, and Mrs. Edward Austen, which are headed *Verses to rhyme with 'Rose'* (Brabourne's edition of the *Letters* (1884), ii. 341–4). Three other poems in the manuscript are by Jane Austen, 'On Sir Home Popham's Sentence, April 1807' and two to Miss Bigg (*Minor Works*, pp. 446–7).

[4] Reproduced in *Volume the Second*.

[5] *Life*, p. 107. Eliza is referred to very guardedly in the *Life*; but from her letters we have a full picture of her powerful and fascinating character (see below, Appendix, pp. 140–2).

an evening's entertainment on a more modest scale they would put on their own rhyming charades;[1] or members of the family would read aloud, Mr. Austen from some popular work and the younger people from their own compositions. Jane Austen's pieces, with their fragile, often allusive humour, were designed for such an intimate hearing. She could depend on the full understanding of her listeners. We, as readers outside the family circle, a century and a half later, cannot hope to enjoy this knowledge of books and people familiar to the household, and for the most part the references are sunk too deeply for us to identify biographical details or parody of specific works.

Sometimes the ground of shared experience, either in literature or life, may have been very narrow, a secret between Jane Austen and the relation or friend to whom the work was dedicated. Inside the front cover of *Volume the First* is stuck a scrap of paper on which Cassandra has written: 'For my Brother Charles, I think I recollect that a few of the trifles in this Vol: were written expressly for his amusement.' In fact two of the sixteen pieces are dedicated to him and, of the remaining fourteen, twelve are addressed to various members of the family and friends. Although Jane Austen was parodying the form and style of the conventional dedication, adopting a grandiloquent manner and a tone of mock gratitude or humility, in several cases we are able to identify a reference within the work which makes its dedication especially appropriate. For example, 'Frederic & Elfrida' is dedicated to Martha Lloyd, 'As a small testimony of the gratitude I feel for your late generosity to me in finishing my muslin Cloak'.[2] In the 'novel' there is a corresponding reference to 'the different excellencies of Indian & English Muslins'.[3] 'The Adventures of Mr. Harley',[4] dedicated to the Midshipman Francis Austen, tells of a hero who obtains a chaplaincy on a man-of-war, thus neatly combining the Austen family professions of church and navy.

[1] Three of Jane Austen's charades are included in a collection printed at the end of *Personal Aspects*, pp. 157–69.
[2] *Volume the First*, p. 4.
[3] p. 9.   [4] p. 73.

In addition to the individual relationship implied by personal dedication all these works are connected to a greater or lesser extent with the general activities of the family. Occasionally, as in the 'History', there are open references to relations, friends, and to details of common knowledge.[1] In 'The three Sisters' Mary Stanhope insists that her husband-to-be build a theatre and put on Mrs. Cowley's *Which is the Man* for the opening performance; this lively play had provided the Christmas entertainment at Steventon in 1787. A more important and distant episode of family history is echoed at the opening of 'Catharine', where we learn that the recently orphaned Cecilia Wynne had been sent to Bengal to find a rich husband.[2] In 1752 Jane Austen's aunt, Philadelphia Austen, likewise a penniless orphan, had been shipped out to Madras to make a similar marriage. Her story was well known to the family, and with her daughter Eliza she was a frequent visitor to her brother's Rectory. 'Catharine' was dedicated to Cassandra in August 1792, only eight months after Philadelphia's death. In giving this account of Cecilia's fate Jane Austen was perhaps making a gesture of sympathy and respect.

Our awareness of the family background is also reinforced by scenes presented so vividly that they seem to carry the impress of reality. Such a ring of truth, amongst material that is not so sharply focused, suggests, for example, that the events and conversations in 'Letter the third' and 'Letter the fourth'[3] are taken from incidents within Jane Austen's personal observation. Perhaps these are the living dramas of the parish, the history of her neighbours, now recorded and re-created for all the family to remember and laugh over. But to a large extent this historical content has passed away with the memory and lives of the Rectory audience. Its recovery is a task for the historian and biographer. For our purpose it is enough to be aware of this stratum of lost or hidden meaning; the principal and permanent entertainment is that of burlesque, which still carries much of its original point.

[1] *Volume the Second*, notes to pp. 140, 141, 142.
[2] *Volume the Third*, pp. 34–35.   [3] *Volume the Second*, pp. 164–77.

Within her home life the important literary influence was that of her reading. In the *Biographical Notice* Henry Austen writes, 'It is difficult to say at what age she was not intimately acquainted with the merits and defects of the best essays and novels in the English language.'[1] Even allowing for the partiality of this account we can be sure that Jane Austen was encouraged to read extensively throughout her childhood.

Henry describes her father (again, perhaps over-warmly) as 'not only a profound scholar, but possessing a most exquisite taste in every species of literature',[2] a taste no less catholic than liberal. In 1798 Jane Austen wrote to her sister[3] that Mr. Austen was reading a newly-published Gothic story by Francis Lathom, *The Midnight Bell* (1798), one of the novels mentioned in *Northanger Abbey*. Under the guidance of her father and brothers not only did she know something of Shakespeare, Pope, Fielding, Richardson, Sterne, Johnson, Sheridan, and Fanny Burney, but she was also acquainted with the minor fiction of the period, not all of which could be classified as polite literature. In the plays performed at the Rectory[4] she met comedy at least as censurable as the topic of *Lovers' Vows*.[5] At Steventon literature was an exciting and amusing activity, to be shared with the whole family; and it is perhaps for this reason that literary experience is so deeply embedded in all her writing.

The reading of great literature (as distinct from the mass of other minor works that she assimilated critically, with amusement and contempt) was a profound experience. At its deepest

---

[1] *Northanger Abbey*, p. 7.   [2] p. 3.   [3] *Letters*, p. 21.

[4] From the *Life* (pp. 63–66) and *Austen Papers* (pp. 126, 138) we can list some of the plays performed at Steventon before 1790. Where these authorities conflict I prefer the *Austen Papers*, which is the likely source for the *Life*. 1784: Sheridan, *The Rivals* (1775); Thomas Franklin, *Matilda* (1775). 1787: Mrs. Centlivre, *The Wonder* (1714); Mrs. Cowley, *Which is the Man* (1782). 1788: ? Garrick, *The Chances* (1773); Garrick, *High Life Above Stairs* (1775). 1789: Townley, *Higʻɪ Life Below Stairs* (1759); Bickerstaffe, *The Sultan* (1775). Jane Austen also knew the part of Mrs. Candour in *The School for Scandal* (1771).

[5] In *Mansfield Park* Jane Austen's views on private theatricals are severely critical in tone—not because she was any less generous-minded than as a child, but because of the bad odour that had lately come to attach to these activities.

level, this influence is not easy to observe in the juvenilia. The impact of great writing upon an undeveloped mind is not to be measured by obvious affinities, borrowings, or allusions. It is a force which works subtly upon the moral temper, touches the imagination, colouring the vision and interpretation of reality. One would judge that the external influences most generally at work in the mature novels are Johnson's moral rationalism, Richardson's intense observation of human conduct, and the judgement of Cowper. In her childhood writing, of course, the influence of these and other authors is registered at a more superficial level. The young girl borrowed freely for her comic situations and characters. Her assurance of style—in the turn of phrase, the structure of sentences, the design of paragraphs, and the handling of dialogue—can be traced back to models such as Fielding, Richardson, Johnson, Sheridan, and Fanny Burney; and in the extensive range of popular fiction (fully surveyed by Dr. Tompkins)[1] she discovered the faults to mock and avoid.

Although sometimes she even turned to parodying her masters, Johnson[2] and Richardson,[3] her principal target was sentimental fiction, popular reading which she was to describe in *Sanditon* as 'The mere Trash of the common Circulating Library'.[4] The rewards of this writing attracted hacks and ambitious amateurs whose work invited ridicule. But the impulse behind Jane Austen's attack was not merely that of amused contempt. With many eighteenth-century critics she believed that the indulgence of emotion was a dangerous example in literature as in life. She also believed that literature is properly a means to truth, and that truth is to be found in the realms of common sense and real life, not in the romantic delusions of sentimentalism.

[1] *The Popular Novel in England, 1770–1800* (1932).
[2] The stream description in 'Love and Friendship' (*Volume the Second*, pp. 42–43) parodies Johnson's description of Glen Sheil, *A Journey to the Western Islands* (1775), 1825, xix. 36. Johnson's highly characteristic manner of thought and style is imitated in 'A Fragment', unfinished and cancelled (*Volume the First*, pp. 131–2).
[3] The poetic diction employed in the description of another stream (there could be some family joke here), *Sir Charles Grandison* (1753–4), 1931, ii. 427, is parodied in 'Frederic & Elfrida' (*Volume the First*, p. 7).
[4] p. 105.

Richardson was the prime example of a writer who had developed the novel of sentiment as a means to explore the truth of society and the human heart. The 1870 *Memoir* testifies that her 'knowledge of Richardson's works was such as no one is likely again to acquire'.[1] By 1791 she had certainly read *Sir Charles Grandison*,[2] and Richardson's novels would have been familiar to the family then as they were to the next generation.[3] Thus in attacking sentimental fiction, beyond mocking its intrinsic defects, she was also measuring it against the positive fact of Richardson's achievement, a standard of value which would be known to her first audience.

Charlotte Smith is the only contemporary novelist whose works are referred to in the juvenilia. Jane Austen had read *Emmeline* (1788) by November 1791,[4] and *Ethelinde* (1789) by August 1792.[5] But the absence of other particular references is no handicap to our understanding of the burlesque. Indeed, my impression is that for much of the time Jane Austen had no specific works in mind, but was aiming at the entire range of sentimental fiction. She brings together all the characteristic figures, devices, and plots, their weaknesses made glaringly apparent in the brief compass of her little tales or treated at greater length in 'Love and Friendship'. Richardson's imitators lacked his technique and imaginative powers. They resorted to time-worn stories, usually variations on the 'Clarissa' situation, with melodramatic action and ridiculous, ill-constructed plots turning on disguises, mistaken identities, mislaid letters, and similar mysteries, some of them unexplained to the end. The heroines are type figures, often of romantic ancestry or mysterious origin. What they lack in formal education is made up for by intuition, the endowment of a delicate sensibility, which enables them to discriminate between the true friend (the confidant with whom all secrets are to be shared—a structural

[1] pp. 109–10.
[2] Allusions occur in *Volume the First*, p. 26; *Volume the Third*, p. 18.
[3] Hill, p. 240.
[4] Allusions in *Volume the Second*, pp. 137, 143; *Volume the Third*, p. 44.
[5] Mentioned in *Volume the Third*, pp. 44–45.

necessity in the epistolary novel) and the coarse, insensitive people
of everyday life. Much of their time is spent in exchanging life-
stories with other sentimental girls who have tales of equal distress to communicate—pathetic accounts of jealous guardians,
arranged marriages, pursuing suitors, and persecuted lovers.
Their sensibility is demonstrated in a number of conventional
signs or poses: pity by tears, compassion by sighs and exclama-
tions, modesty by blushes and lowered eyes, contrition by
kneeling, and shock by swoons or madness. This theatrical
conduct is matched in the rhapsodical tones of the dialogue and
in the rhetorical level of the narrative style. As Jane Austen
observed of *Clarentine* (1798, by Sarah Burney), the stories
written to this pattern were 'full of unnatural conduct &
forced difficulties'.[1] There were many such novels, for certain
features of sentimental fiction are common to historical and
Gothic romances, to the so-called propaganda novels and the
novels of purpose. Even Fanny Burney's heroines are cast in
the sentimental mould.

Jane Austen's critical response to this literature was not
wholly spontaneous. Throughout the eighteenth century there
was considerable opposition to the extravagance of sentimental
fiction and the wildness of romances, with their power to capti-
vate a young mind. She must have been familiar with the confession of Mrs. Shirley in *Sir Charles Grandison*. Speaking of the
influence of French romances Mrs. Shirley admits that in her
youth she 'was over-run with the absurdities of that unnatural
kind of writing. . . . I had very high ideas of first impressions:
eternal constancy: of Love raised to a pitch of idolatry.'[2] The
most amusing burlesque of this romantic delusion was *The
Female Quixote* (1752), by Mrs. Charlotte Lennox. Jane Austen
wrote to Cassandra in 1807 that the Steventon household had
been reading this book for their 'evening amusement; to me a
very high one, as I find the work quite equal to what I remembered it';[3] probably she was remembering it from childhood.

[1] In a letter to Cassandra, 8 February 1807 (*Letters*, p. 180).
[2] Oxford (1931), vi. 223.   [3] *Letters*, p. 173.

The situation in 'Edgar & Emma', where the heroine, in search of a confidant, turns in desperation to the footman,[1] is perhaps a memory of Mrs. Lennox's heroine, Arabella, who may also have been in Jane Austen's mind when she was writing of Margaret Lesley in 'Lesley Castle'. In Mrs. Smith's *Emmeline*, another book she knew well, Fitz Edward is sharply rebuked by Stafford for his melodramatic language: 'Does a modern man of fashion pretend to talk of madness and death? You certainly imagine, Sir, that you are speaking to some romantic inhabitant of a Welch provincial town, whose ideas are drawn from a circulating library.'[2] In 'Love and Friendship' Sir Edward rebukes his son in similar terms for using language equally melodramatic.[3] The prime example of one 'whose ideas are drawn from a circulating library' is Lydia Languish in *The Rivals*, which was produced at Steventon in 1784. Jane Austen also knew Sheridan's other attack in *The School for Scandal*, where there is a brilliant satire upon Joseph Surface, the sentimentalist hypocrite.[4] It is from these burlesques and literary attacks of this kind that Jane Austen learned to develop her own method.

Even in childhood she must have been aware of the serious moral arguments levelled against sentimental fiction; if from no other source, she would have come to hear of them through the family. Her brothers James and Henry edited *The Loiterer*, an Oxford periodical that ran for sixty numbers between January 1789 and March 1790. Some of the issues may have been planned and written at Steventon. With our knowledge of life at the Rectory we can be almost certain that she would have heard or read her brothers' contributions, perhaps even making suggestions at the time of writing. This she would have enjoyed, for in addition to providing a commentary on Oxford life, *The*

---

[1] *Volume the First*, p. 58.   [2] 1788, i. 117.
[3] *Volume the Second*, p. 11.
[4] Sheridan may also have served Jane Austen in 'The Mystery' (*Volume the First*, pp. 100–3), which satirizes the device of conveying tracts of information through dialogue. The conversation in Scene Two deals in hints, mysteries, and unrevealed facts, dramatic devices also ridiculed in a similar conversation between Raleigh and Hatton in *The Critic* (II. i). This scene is referred to in the 'History' (*Volume the Second*, p. 145).

Loiterer is largely concerned with the literature of sensibility, warning against its excesses, in serious Johnsonian prose, and mocking it through burlesque stories and letters. In no. 47 Henry blames the sentimental novel for the spread of a 'degenerate and sickly refinement'.[1] He goes on to warn his readers that those who follow the example of the sentimental heroines 'will be tortured by the poignant delicacy of their own feelings, and fall the Martyrs to their own Susceptibility'.[2] Perhaps Jane Austen recalled Henry's warning of December 1789, at the time her own compositions were evolving. Six months later 'Love and Friendship' (which occurs as a phrase in no. 27) was completed, and we find the heroine echoing Henry's words: 'A sensibility too tremblingly alive to every affliction of my Freinds, my Acquaintance and particularly to every affliction of my own, was my only fault, if a fault it could be called.'[3]

The title of the Austens' periodical may have been imitated from *The Lounger*, Henry Mackenzie's weekly which ran from 1785 to 1787. Jane Austen knew of *The Mirror*,[4] Mackenzie's first set of essays, published in 1779 and 1780. In both these papers she could have followed his attack upon the over-refined sensibility which precludes determined action and gives freedom to the play of every emotion and whim. Above all he feared that civilized values and personal rectitude were endangered by the influence that such a pattern of life might exert.[5]

Jane Austen probably met this train of thought in her everyday reading, and heard it discussed among her elders, perhaps heatedly, but more probably as a topic of amusement. In choosing the sophisticated form of burlesque she was taking her place in a flourishing tradition; and in attacking sentimental fiction she was again following common practice. In her handling of conventional material and methods we see the power of her mind, a critical sense directed by the impulse of creation. And while the later juvenilia are increasingly concerned with

[1] p. 3.   [2] p. 5.
[3] *Volume the Second*, p. 6.   [4] *Northanger Abbey*, p. 241.
[5] See especially *Lounger*, no. 20; *Mirror*, no. 101.

the realistic treatment of domestic themes and situations, literary satire was to remain an important source of entertainment
and a considerable element of meaning in the mature novels,
perhaps partly in answer to those of her family and friends
who preferred the sparkling comedy of *Pride and Prejudice* to
the more serious style and tone of *Mansfield Park*.[1] She was
always concerned to entertain this, her closest audience, whose
encouragement was the spur of her wit, and whose presence
was felt throughout her life.

(III)

The original manuscripts of the juvenilia have not survived.
What we have is a collection of transcripts made by Jane Austen
in the three notebooks. The transcription of this material, as
we can see from the writing, was carried out at various times
over a long period. Some entries are made very carefully in
a beautiful copperplate hand, with errors neatly expunged.
This would indicate that Jane Austen was preparing a collection to be circulated and read among the family. Many pieces,
however, are entered hastily in a less carefully formed script,
the cancellations and corrections added with no regard to the
fair-copy appearance of the notebooks. Here it would seem that
she was merely collecting her early pieces as a record of work,
perhaps for the convenience of reading aloud. She may have destroyed the originals when they had been copied; or perhaps they
were dispersed among the relations and friends to whom they
were dedicated. Whatever the explanation, no originals survive.

We are able to form a chronology of composition around
four pieces dated by Jane Austen herself. The earliest of these
is 'Love and Friendship', inscribed at the end, 13 June 1790.[2]
This is a developed, large-scale burlesque, clearly of later composition than the short pieces in *Volume the First*, which, for all
their sharpness, have a larger element of childish nonsense and
fantasy. Probably Jane Austen was thinking of these works in

---

[1] See her collection of *Opinions*, reprinted in *Plan of a Novel*, pp. 13–17.
[2] *Volume the Second*, p. 66.

1817 when she warned Caroline Austen to stop writing until she was sixteen. She told her twelve-year-old niece 'that she had herself often wished she had read more, and written less in the corresponding years of her own life'.[1] This implies that she was already writing in 1787, soon after her return from the Abbey School, Reading, to which she was sent with Cassandra in 1783.[2] According to the 1871 *Memoir* her childhood tales 'had amounted to a considerable number by the time she was sixteen',[3] in December 1791. After this, the latest date we can put to the composition of any of the juvenilia is 3 June 1793, written on the final page of *Volume the First*.[4]

Within this period of five or six years three items, in addition to 'Love and Friendship', can be dated by a specific entry on the manuscript: 'The History of England', 26 November 1791, in *Volume the Second*; 'Catharine', August 1792, in *Volume the Third*; 'A Fragment', 2 June 1793, in *Volume the First*. The letters in 'Lesley Castle' are dated 3 January to 13 April 1792, a period which may correspond to that of their composition. Five more pieces can be dated approximately on external evidence: 'Jack & Alice' and 'The Adventures of Mr. Harley' in *Volume the First* are both dedicated to Francis Austen, 'Midshipman on board his Majesty's ship the Perseverance',[5] in which he served from 1788 until November 1791. 'Henry and Eliza', also in *Volume the First*, and 'A Collection of Letters' in *Volume the Second* are both dedicated to Miss Cooper, a childhood friend who married Thomas Williams on 11 December 1792. 'The beautifull Cassandra' in *Volume the First* is mentioned in the dedication to 'Catharine', which places its composition before August 1792. The remaining undated pieces can

---

[1] Quoted in the 1871 *Memoir*, p. 45.

[2] Following the *Life* (p. xiii) Dr. Chapman dates her departure from the school 1784 or 1785 (*Facts and Problems*, p. 175). Mr. T. Edward Carpenter has drawn my attention to entries in the ledgers of Messrs. Hoare that record payments made by Mr. Austen to Mrs. Latournelle (headmistress of the Abbey School) in August 1785, February 1786, and January 1787. Unless these are back-payments it appears that Jane Austen attended the school for a longer period than has been thought.

[3] p. 42.   [4] p. 138.   [5] pp. 20, 73.

be placed on the evidence of style, which I discuss in Chapter 2. Meanwhile, I suggest the following order of composition, with months where these are known:

1787–90	'Frederic & Elfrida', 'Jack & Alice', 'Edgar & Emma', 'Henry and Eliza', 'Mr. Harley', 'Sir William Mountague', 'Mr. Clifford', 'The beautifull Cassandra', 'Amelia Webster', 'The Visit', 'The Mystery' (all *Volume the First*).
1790 June	'Love and Friendship' (*Volume the Second*).
1791 November	'The History of England' (*Volume the Second*).
	'Collection of Letters' (*Volume the Second*).
1792	'Lesley Castle' (*Volume the Second*).
	'The three Sisters' (*Volume the First*).
	'Evelyn' (*Volume the Third*).
August	'Catharine' (*Volume the Third*).
1793	'Scraps' (*Volume the Second*).
June	'Detached pieces' (*Volume the First*).
	'Ode to Pity' (*Volume the First*).

For the dating of the transcription we have to depend on evidence of the manuscript hand. This cannot be an exact method, but it provides us with an approximate relative order for the entry of the material.

In *Volume the First* variations in the hand show that the re-copying was carried out over a long period, beginning in childhood, possibly soon after the composition of the earliest pieces. Dr. Chapman notes that for much of the manuscript the writing is 'somewhat large and not completely formed, becomes smaller and more mature towards the end, and in the concluding pages is not unlike the hand which wrote *The Watsons* not earlier than 1803'.[1] With development in the hand there comes a corresponding change in the style of the pieces. The first eleven items, entered in the child's writing, belong clearly to what we can identify as the earliest stage in Jane Austen's authorship. After this the remainder of the notebook is of later entry and the

---

[1] Preface, p. vii.

material of later composition. What Dr. Chapman describes as the 'smaller and more mature hand' is almost identical with that Jane Austen was using in a letter of 1796.[1]

There is also a wide variation of hand in *Volume the Second*. Some entries (e.g. the dedications to 'Love and Friendship' and 'Scraps'[2]) are made in a fine, beautifully formed copperplate script. 'Love and Friendship' is written in the 'middle' hand, similar to that of 'The three Sisters' in *Volume the First*. By contrast, whereas among 'Scraps' at the end of the notebook the 'Comedy'[3] is in the calligraphic hand, other pages are scribbled untidily in what appears to be a later script.[4] This suggests that Jane Austen returned to complete these entries hurriedly, perhaps long after they were begun.

On the first leaf of *Volume the Third* is written 'Jane Austen— May 6th 1792'. This date probably refers to the time that she received the notebook, perhaps as a gift from her father as *Volume the Second* had been. Most of the notebook is entered in the 'middle' hand, although there is evidence that changes and additions were being made as late as 1809. In 'Catharine'[5] a reference to 'Seccar's explanation of the Catechism' is changed to 'Coelebs in Search of a Wife' (by Hannah More), which Jane Austen was writing of to Cassandra in January 1809,[6] the month of its publication.

Jane Austen's continued interest in this material so long after its original composition is to be explained by its importance as a kind of traditional family literature, known and loved from the author's readings. In a letter of 1814[7] she could expect Cassandra to take an allusive reference to 'Love and Friendship', written twenty-four years earlier. Further evidence of the lively family interest is the addition to 'Evelyn', three leaves inserted at the end of the notebook[8] in continuation of that tale. This entry was made and initialed by Anna Austen, in her married name, Lefroy. She became Benjamin Lefroy's wife in 1814, so

---

[1] Letter 5, 5 September 1796. [2] Manuscript, pp. 1, 237.
[3] Ibid., pp. 241–4. [4] Ibid., pp. 240, 245.
[5] p. 111. [6] Letters 65, 66.
[7] *Letters*, p. 397. [8] *Volume the Third*, pp. 129–32.

the addition was made at least twenty-two years after Jane Austen began the story in 1792. Perhaps another member of the family was responsible for interpolations to this same notebook, where 'Evelyn', left unfinished by Jane Austen, is completed in a further six pages,[1] and 'Catharine', likewise unfinished, was continued for another four paragraphs.[2] The difference in handwriting, peculiarities of spelling, and the weakness of style in these passages convince me that Jane Austen neither composed nor transcribed them.[3] Although we are unable to identify the hand, this is probably the work of one of her story-writing nephews or nieces who might well have enjoyed access to the notebook when Jane Austen was living at Chawton after 1809.

The presence of alterations and additions, some of them perhaps made by members of the family, might suggest that Jane Austen herself improved the originals, either during the course of transcribing them or in revision. But there is, in fact, no sign that she did carry out any general scheme of improvement. She was probably concerned to keep a faithful record of her earliest work, and had little time for extensive rewriting. The manuscripts reveal that the entries are mere copying, automatic transcription. The verbal omissions, repetitions, and inconsistencies are the errors commonly associated with this kind of work. They are not the mistakes of a writer who is thinking critically about her material. The alterations are largely those of current correction, to eliminate obvious mistakes in copying. They rarely point to the creative process which we can identify in the changes to the manuscripts of *The Watsons* and *Sanditon*. The most important signs of later revision are cancellations,[4] modifications rather than improvements. As far as can be judged we are dealing with transcripts which follow their originals closely.

[1] *Volume the Third*, pp. 23–27. Manuscript, p. 21, l. 5 to p. 27.

[2] pp. 125–8. Manuscript, p. 124, l. 16 to p. 127.

[3] For a full discussion of this evidence see my note, 'Interpolations to Jane Austen's "Volume the Third" ', *Notes and Queries* ccvii (May, 1962), 185–7.

[4] E.g., *Volume the First*, pp. 33, 93, 114, and see my discussion in 'The Manuscript of Jane Austen's Volume the First', *The Library* (Fifth Series), xvii. 3 (September 1962), 231–7.

The three notebooks seem to be an almost complete collection of the early work. Only *Volume the Second* is imperfect, twelve sheets having been removed.[1] Little can be missing; there is no break in the entries, and the manuscript was paginated and the contents page drawn up after the removal of all but one of the sheets. The only other hint of lost material is suggested by the wording of the dedications to 'The Visit' and 'Lesley Castle'. This opens the possibility that two little plays and some early 'novels' may not have been entered in the notebooks.[2] Yet their absence is not a serious loss; as it is, we have a sufficiently wide picture of Jane Austen's childhood writing to make such slight gaps relatively unimportant.

[1] See *Volume the Second*, Notes on the Missing Sheets, p. 209.

[2] See my discussion of this point in 'Jane Austen's Juvenilia: The Question of Completeness', *Notes and Queries*, ccix (May 1964), 180-1.

2

A CRITICAL STUDY OF THE JUVENILIA

ARECURRENT theme in Jane Austen's writing is the need to distinguish between reality and illusion, to explore and discriminate among conditions of true and false vision, a purpose which Sir Walter Scott recognized in *Emma*. Reviewing the work in 1816[1] he drew a comparison between two kinds of novel: what he called 'the modern novel', of which *Emma* was representative, through which runs 'the current of ordinary life',[2] to be admired for its fidelity to common experience; the other kind, its opposite, the sentimental romance, in which 'the reader expected to pursue a course of adventures of a nature more interesting and extraordinary than those which occur in his own life, or that of his next door neighbours'.[3] In this type of fiction 'The novelist professed to give an imitation of nature, but it was, as the French say, *la belle nature*. Human beings, indeed were presented, but in the most sentimental mood, and with minds purified by a sensibility which often verged on extravagance.'[3] In *Emma* he noticed the delicate hint of literary satire, 'cross purposes enough (were the novel of a more romantic cast) for cutting half the men's throats and breaking all the women's hearts'.[4] Throughout the book Jane Austen plays quietly upon the devices and situations of the novels of 'romantic cast', adjusting them to a story whose drama and distresses are domestic, mild and unemphatic, and which arise largely out of Emma's wilful imagination, her misjudgements and interferences. Eventually the heroine comes to learn through experience that her fancies and romantic speculations are far less satisfying than the reality around her,

---

[1] *Quarterly Review*, xiv (for October 1815, published March 1816), 188–201.   [2] Ibid., p. 189.   [3] Ibid.   [4] Ibid., p. 196.

which possesses an imaginative power and enchantment of its own.

Such positive reflections on the quality of true and false vision are not to be adduced directly from the juvenilia, although some sense of this purpose, however faint and undefined, is present from the beginning. In the earliest burlesques Jane Austen mimicked and ridiculed *la belle nature* of popular fiction, amused at the novelists' picture of life and contemptuous of their faults of style and technique, which she parodied and set off with passages of good writing and glancing reminders of the world of common sense. Later, in 'Love and Friendship', she brought the realm of sentimental illusion into conflict with the conditions of ordinary life. Among the last of the juvenilia the most important works are those in which the burlesque element is subordinated to realistic social comedy. In this line of development we can divide the juvenilia into three groups: the pieces written between 1787 and 1790; the two middle works 'Love and Friendship', 1790, and 'The History of England', 1791; and finally the works of 1792–3.

(1)

The Earliest Juvenilia, 1787–1790

The earliest juvenilia are the work of a high-spirited child set on amusement, delighting in knockabout farce, fanciful extravagance, solemn nonsense, and word-play. For all its exuberance the wit is shrewdly applied in exposing the false values and absurd conventions of sentimental fiction, and in general the flaws of bad writing. In these pieces are crowded together many characteristic devices of the popular novel: the abundance of confidants, the recital of life-stories, the melodramatic succession of catastrophes, the interpolation of songs and poems, the egotistic heroines, the rhapsodical style, the technical weaknesses of clumsy plotting, improbable action, neglect of time scale, inconsequence and digression. The most distinctive feature of this burlesque method is the manipulation of style. At one extreme, as in 'Jack & Alice', Jane Austen mimics the inflated rhetoric, the rhythms and cliché diction of sentimental writing:

Thus fell the amiable & lovely Lucy whose Life had been marked by no crime, and stained by no blemish but her imprudent departure from her Aunts, & whose death was sincerely lamented by every one who knew her.[1]

Playing upon the reader's familiarity with this stylistic norm Jane Austen opens 'Frederic & Elfrida' with a neatness and precision of phrasing that sets off the absurdity of the subject-matter:

The Uncle of Elfrida was the Father of Frederic; in other words, they were first cousins by the Father's side. Being both born in one day & both brought up at one school, it was not wonderfull that they should look on each other with something more than bare politeness. They loved with mutual sincerity but were both determined not to transgress the rules of Propriety by owning their attachment, either to the object beloved, or to any one else.[2]

Later in this story there is another type of burlesque incongruity. An account of 'the amiable Rebecca'[3] begins unremarkably; it appears to be the type description of the conventional heroine; yet we soon discover that she is no flawless young woman but an object of physical repulsion.

The most amusing effects are gained when Jane Austen exploits the disparity between broad farcical comedy in the action and the studied formality of the sentimental language and behaviour of the characters. In 'Frederic & Elfrida' Charlotte is sitting with her aunt when she receives the old gentleman's proposal:

Scarcely were they seated as usual, in the most affectionate manner in one chair, than the Door suddenly opened & an aged gentleman with a sallow face & old pink Coat, partly by intention & partly thro' weakness was at the feet of the lovely Charlotte, declaring his attachment to her & beseeching her pity in the most moving manner. Not being able

---

[1] *Volume the First*, p. 51.   [2] p. 5.   [3] p. 9.

to resolve to make any one miserable, she consented to become his wife; where upon the Gentleman left the room & all was quiet.[1]

The comic effect is markedly theatrical. In the same way Lady Williams's account of her education begins in conventional terms, and ends in the manner of a stage farce:

'Miss Dickins was an excellent Governess. She instructed me in the Paths of Virtue; under her tuition I daily became more amiable, & might perhaps by this time have nearly attained perfection, had not my worthy Preceptoress been torn from my arms, e'er I had attained my seventeenth year. I never shall forget her last words. 'My dear Kitty she said Good nightt'ye." I never saw her afterwards' continued Lady Williams wiping her eyes, 'She eloped with the Butler the same night.'[2]

In these sudden descents of language and action her audience would be reminded that Fielding, Smollett, Sterne, and the popular dramatists provided similar comic melodrama to ridicule the idealization of impulsive love and elopement.

But the clearest hint of Jane Austen's future power is not related directly to her methods of burlesque. It is glimpsed, rather, in an occasional succinct aphorism or finely-turned comment, as in the description of Lady Williams—'a widow with a handsome Jointure & the remains of a very handsome face';[3] and in Lady Williams's advice to Alice—'Preserve yourself from a first Love & you need not fear a second';[4] or in the words of Mr. Johnson—'I expect nothing more in my wife than my wife will find in me—Perfection.'[5] This command of style is shown on a larger scale at the opening to chapter 2 of 'Edgar & Emma', with its pointed phrasing, the balance and variety of sentence-patterns, the neatness of structure, and the quiet, dismissive irony of the concluding lines:

The news of their arrival being quickly spread throughout the Country, brought them in a few Days visits of congratulation from every family in it.
Amongst the rest came the inhabitants of Willmot Lodge a beautifull Villa not far from Marlhurst. Mr. Willmot was the representative

[1] p. 13.　　[2] pp. 28–29.　　[3] p. 21.　　[4] p. 28.　　[5] p. 46.

of a very ancient Family & possessed besides his paternal Estate a considerable share in a Lead mine & a ticket in the Lottery. His Lady was an agreable Woman. Their Children were too numerous to be particularly described; it is sufficient to say that in general they were virtuously inclined & not given to any wicked ways.[1]

The tone of this passage catches the note of amusement with which we imagine the Austens to have viewed the arrival of new families in their own neighbourhood. This is 'the current of real life', the order of reality in which one might also observe the animosity between Alice Johnson and Lady Williams. In the figure of Lady Williams, a type of Mrs. Candour, Jane Austen explores the limits of indulging spite and insolence within the forms of polite society. This is an account of manners as true to life as Charlotte's behaviour (in 'Frederic & Elfrida') when her friend Rebecca comes fishing for praise:

Charlotte, who perfectly understood the meaning of her freind's speech, was too good-temper'd & obliging to refuse her, what she knew she wished,—a compliment; & they parted the best freinds in the world.[2]

In these pieces Jane Austen reveals herself as a child of the eighteenth century. If anyone is surprised or even shocked that a young girl was ready to joke about deformity, injury, death, drunkenness, child-bearing, and illegitimacy, it should be remembered that much of this vigorous humour derives from traditions of fiction and stage comedy with which the Steventon household was familiar. Writing for such an intimate audience Jane Austen could express herself here as freely as in her letters to Cassandra, with no thought that these private jokes would ever go beyond the family, let alone be published and discussed.

(II)

The Middle Work, 1790–1791

The burlesque criticism of sentimental fiction is continued in 'Love and Friendship', a brisk and sustained comedy on a large

---

[1] pp. 56–57.   [2] p. 12.

scale. There is a good deal of playful nonsense and allusive humour, obviously designed to amuse the children; yet, as a whole, the work is far more sophisticated than anything in the earliest juvenilia, and provides entertainment not wholly dependent upon burlesque. The heroine's narrative point of view, maintained throughout the letters, controls a variety of material and gives the work an overall unity and form.

Laura provides a full exposition of sentimental doctrine, which stands condemned, not only in its own terms, but also by direct accusation voiced within the story by a number of common-sense, sceptical figures. When Edward, her husband, delivers an outburst of sentimental 'Manliness'—that is, a refusal to accept his father's authority—Sir Edward replies, 'Where Edward in the name of wonder . . . did you pick up this unmeaning Gibberish? You have been studying Novels I suspect.'[1] His sister is equally unimpressed by Edward's bombast, and meets his declarations with ironic banter. Later, we see that stealing—like parasitism, hypocrisy, and illegitimacy—is an occasion for the sentimentalist's self-glorification, an assertion of individual superiority to laws and normal conventions. But real life breaks in upon this delusion. Augustus is imprisoned, and Laura and Sophia are ejected from Macdonald Hall.

Throughout the work a critical relationship is maintained between this behaviour and the conditions of the sober world. The sentimentalists come to learn that prudence can be more profitable than the extravagance of their code. Sophia, indulging her sensibility, faints so long and so often in the falling dew that she succumbs to a fatal chill. From her death-bed she warns Laura to 'beware of fainting-fits';[2] Laura follows this advice and survives. At the end of her account she is able to write of her retirement to a romantic Highland village. There, in the manner of a lachrymose heroine, she can 'indulge in a melancholy solitude, my unceasing Lamentations'.[3] But this retreat is possible only because she has accepted an annuity from her father-in-law, Sir Edward, whom she earlier saw as a tyrannical

[1] *Volume the Second*, p. 11.   [2] p. 52.   [3] p. 65.

and unfeeling villain. So the sentimentalist is ready to compromise with reality, if only to heed its warnings and accept its gifts.

In this way Jane Austen not only displays and laughs at sentimental conduct but on a more serious level questions its motives. It is shown up as nothing more than an expedient code of self-indulgence, a form of egotistical snobbery. Almost imperceptibly burlesque becomes a satire on affectation. Later Jane Austen translated this theme into realistic social comedy. The display of feeling put on by the Steele sisters is inspired by opportunism, in contrast to the genuine temperamental sensibility of Marianne Dashwood. But in 1790 the comedy was swift and hard. Jane Austen was simply concerned to analyse and ridicule a particular kind of literary pretension, not to portray the force of real emotion in a sympathetic figure.

Her other purpose in this work was to illustrate the mishandling of the letter as a narrative form. Richardson's success in the epistolary novel had shown how well it was suited to the intense study of the human consciousness, the revelation of states of mind and feeling. Although it was less effective for telling a story, by the 1780's and 1790's it had become the most popular method for all kinds of fiction, probably because of its simplicity as a narrative vehicle. At the opening of 'Love and Friendship' the occasion of the correspondence is made to appear clumsy and ludicrous, and in the rest of the work the highly eventful story exposes the limitations of the letter for dealing with such material. Jane Austen follows the usual practice, with a series of letters 'in continuation' or 'from the same to the same', interrupting the narrative flow as little as possible, merely using the letter as a structural device to replace division by chapters. Her burlesque distortion is to open and close Laura's correspondence in an arbitrary manner, breaking the story in the middle of action as no conventional chapter division would do. This is not, however, an outright rejection of the epistolary convention. Jane Austen acknowledged its use for certain kinds of material, and within two years was experimenting seriously with the letter as a device for social observation and character drawing.

Sentimental fiction was not the only kind of writing in which reality might be distorted or concealed by the colouring of romance. This was also happening in popular historical works. In historical fiction and children's books flights of imagination could be a welcome relief. Even in works of pretension accounts of the established facts were frequently enlivened with anecdotes and other less reliable forms of evidence, and the style was appropriately lightened. For example, in Goldsmith's *History of England* (1764) the description of Anne Boleyn is in the manner of any hack novelist: 'Her features were regular, mild, and attractive, her stature elegant, though below the middle size, while her wit and vivacity exceeded even her other allurements.'[1] And the account of the suicide of Essex in Dalrymple's *Memoirs of Great Britain and Ireland* (1771–88) provoked Johnson's exclamation: 'All history, so far as it is not supported by contemporary evidence is romance.'[2] Jane Austen plays with this view in *Northanger Abbey*, where Catherine Morland is surprised to find histories so tedious, for she had supposed most of the heroes' speeches, thoughts, and designs 'must be invention, and invention is what delights me in other books'.[3]

'The History of England' attacks popular historical writing of this kind, where all too often the attempt to refurbish borrowed material has turned fact into the semblance of fiction. Like 'Love and Friendship' the 'History' is not a parody of specific works, although it is clear that both Goldsmith's *History* and the *Abridgement* (1774) were among the chosen targets. The marginal comments in Jane Austen's copy of the *History* reveal her indignation at Goldsmith's bias against the Stuarts, which she answers in the 'History', announcing defiantly that it was written 'to prove the innocence of the Queen of Scotland, which I flatter myself with having effectually done, and to abuse

[1] ii. 353.   [2] *Tour* (1785), ed. R. W. Chapman (1924), p. 432.
[3] p. 108.

Elizabeth'.[1] Her objection to abridgements is well known from the complaint in *Northanger Abbey*: that these works enjoy a reputation denied to the novel—how undeservedly, she illustrates in the opening to her entry for Edward IV,[2] a close mimicry of the corresponding section in Goldsmith's *Abridgement*.[3] Another target was the considerable branch of historical fiction devoted to embroidery upon the life of Mary Stuart. A notable and absurd fantasy of this kind was *The Recess* (1765) by Mrs. Lee, in which the friendship between Mary and Norfolk is represented as a romantic liaison, a fancy echoed in Jane Austen's account.

The manner of popular historical writing is taken to an extravagant conclusion. The historians treated the figures of the past as if their characters and feelings were fully known. Accordingly, Jane Austen writes of sovereigns and great men with an air of careless familiarity, as if they were figures of her own time. Richard III is 'a very respectable Man';[4] Charles I an 'amiable Monarch';[5] the Catholics 'did not behave like Gentlemen to the protestants';[6] 'and even Sir Henry Percy tho' certainly the best bred Man of the party, had none of that general politeness which is so universally pleasing'.[7] These judgements belong to the drawing-room, to the historical ignorance of Mrs. Stanley in 'Catharine'.[8] In the same way historical events are treated as the occurrences of everyday life. Joan of Arc 'made such a *row* among the English';[9] Richard III 'made a great fuss about getting the Crown';[10] and in the reign of Henry IV 'the Prince of Wales came and took away the crown'.[11] As a foil to this slangy colloquialism, in writing of Mary Stuart Jane Austen adopts an elevated mock-formal style with rhetorical appeals to the reader, in striking contrast to the rest of the work, where in general the tone is jaunty, the manner inconsequential, with a purely verbal appearance of cause and effect, such as we find in the entry for Henry IV:

[1] *Volume the Second*, p. 148.   [2] p. 131.   [3] p. 155.
[4] p. 132.   [5] p. 146.   [6] p. 144.
[7] pp. 144–5.   [8] *Volume the Third*, pp. 47–48.
[9] *Volume the Second*, p. 130.   [10] p. 132.   [11] p. 129.

Henry the 4th ascended the throne of England much to his own satisfaction in the year 1399, after having prevailed on his cousin & predecessor Richard the 2d, to resign it to him, & to retire for the rest of his Life to Pomfret Castle, where he happened to be murdered. It is to be supposed that Henry was married, since he had certainly four sons, but it is not in my power to inform the Reader who was his Wife. Be this as it may . . . .[1]

This extract is a parody of Goldsmith's worst manner, with its clumsiness and jingling prose. The passage is also significant for the air of casual indifference with which it treats material of human substance and historical importance, subject-matter thereby trivialized. This brings us to the heart of Jane Austen's criticism—that popularized history is as false to the nature of reality as the picture of life given in the sentimental novel, and perhaps more seriously false, for it purports to be dealing with the facts of great men and great events.

At the head of the work Jane Austen announces herself as 'a partial, prejudiced, & ignorant Historian',[2] a pose held so brilliantly and outrageously that we might be forgiven for supposing that the narrative mask was natural to its author. This was a stance demanding considerable powers of detachment. From family memoirs we learn that she was a true supporter of the Stuart cause, and we can judge the strength of this sympathy from the marginalia in her copy of Goldsmith.[3] Probably her feelings were swayed by both personal conviction and family loyalties, for the Leighs, to whom she was related on her mother's side, had sheltered Charles I at Leigh Abbey. Yet so complete is the artistic transformation that her bias appears to be nothing more than rank prejudice, as much a part of the joke and declared in the same terms of irony as the rest of the work, which throughout exhibits the historian's blatant partiality and ignorance. This was a pose Jane Austen could afford to maintain. Writing for her relations and friends she could assume their interest in digressions about Austen family life; she could depend upon

[1] pp. 128–9.   [2] p. 128.
[3] Some of these comments are recorded in *Personal Aspects*, pp. 26–28; for her private attitude see also *My Aunt*, p. 9.

their knowledge of her sources and of Shakespeare; and most important of all she was confident that they would understand the discrepancy between the avowed attitudes of the historian and her own deep sympathies. In this particular situation, as a family writer with a known audience, she was able to put her feelings to the service of burlesque. Her capacity for ironic detachment was inborn; and, as we see here, the conditions of her childhood favoured the cultivation of an aesthetic objectivity, without which her later development in the creation of comic art from her observation of everyday life would not have been possible.

(iii)

The Last of the Juvenilia, 1792–1793

After 'Love and Friendship' and the 'History' the last of the juvenilia read rather disappointingly. They provide nothing comparable in the way of sheer entertainment or artistry. Burlesque comedy, which had fired Jane Austen's imagination, is now relegated to minor pieces, or survives uneasily and intermittently in the longer works, whose satirical view is turned from literature to life. Burlesque would serve for family entertainment, but it could no longer support her interest in character; nor was it suitable as a mode in which to portray scenes of domestic life and polite society. In this setting, the realm of her personal observation, she begins to set down the problems of conduct and judgement that could face any girl in her day-to-day relationships. In particular she was concerned with the testing situations of love and marriage. Following the example of Fanny Burney she introduces a wide range of character types: the timorous simpleton, the witty and perceptive young woman, the well-bred fool, the anxious chaperone, the doting mother, the sentimental heroine, the high-spirited young man, the rich suitor, the mature confidant, and her opposite, the older woman, impertinent and bullying. Whether in burlesque or realistic pieces these figures are exhibited in hard, critical comedy which searches affectation and display, revealing the ignorance, pride, folly, malice, calculation, or self-interest that so often underlie the parade of manners. Only Miss Grenville (in 'Letter the fourth'), and Eloisa Lutterell and Mrs. Marlow (in 'Lesley Castle'), are treated with sympathy. Jane Austen was sketching the surface of personality, noting the particular idiosyncrasy or accent of silliness that distinguishes one fool from another, the little tricks of speech and behaviour through which the qualities of a person's breeding, education, and social position could be read.

The undated 'Collection' of five miscellaneous letters comes immediately after the 'History' in the second manuscript notebook. Its general nature supports a dating late in 1791, or early the following year, certainly before 'Lesley Castle'. In these letters Jane Austen delights in varying her stylistic effects, moving from sentimental eloquence in the burlesque pieces to natural dialogue in the third and fourth letters, where the satire plays upon realistic situations. The first letter, 'From A Mother to her freind', mocks the tradition of the moral and didactic epistle, perfected by Richardson and subsequently used as an editorial device in the periodicals. The other four letters are from 'Young Ladies' in various circumstances of personal stress. The second and fifth are burlesques of sentimental fiction, much in the style of the earliest juvenilia, and 'Letter the fourth', 'From a young Lady rather impertinent to her freind', examines the pose of sentimental friendship.

The remaining letter, no. 3, moves further in the direction of reporting a realistic scene. The literary satire is confined to the title, announcing the heroine as a 'young Lady in distress'd Circumstances'.[1] These are not, as we might suppose, the distresses of a sentimental figure, but the pain and embarrassment of a girl exposed to the insulting patronage of an older woman, Lady Greville, sharp-tongued and censorious. Their antagonism is displayed in three episodes containing a high proportion of dialogue, exchanges in which Lady Greville accuses Maria of being an upstart fortune-hunter, a charge that she resists with

[1] *Volume the Second*, p. 164.

great spirit. The dialogue is sometimes theatrically exaggerated, but this detracts little from its effectiveness as a piece of close and economical reporting. It portrays a clash of temperaments, the malice with which an older, titled woman regards the social aspirations of a penniless and attractive girl, a situation treated again in the encounters of Elizabeth Bennet and Lady Catherine de Bourgh.

In 'Lesley Castle' the epistolary form is used more ambitiously. A loosely connected group of ten letters tells the story of Lady Lesley's marriage and its effect upon her husband's grown-up daughters. Singly the letters are quite successful, but as a whole the work lacks unity. The plot is too slight to provide an organizing centre of interest, and some of the characters stand uneasily between burlesque and realism. This discrepancy is particularly apparent in Charlotte Lutterell, the principal correspondent, who, with Lady Lesley and Mrs. Marlowe, is used to provide the witty and penetrating observation, the ironic point of view from which behaviour and motives are searched.

The revelation of character is made without comment, merely through the style of the correspondents. In the first letter Margaret is given the rhetorical manner of popular fiction. This literary artificiality is immediately contrasted with another artificial manner, that of society slang, at the opening of the next letter, from Charlotte:

I have a thousand excuses to beg for having so long delayed thanking you my dear Peggy for your agreable Letter, which beleive me I should not have deferred doing, had not every moment of my time during the last five weeks been so fully employed in the necessary arrangements for my sisters Wedding, as to allow me no time to devote either to you or myself.[1]

This is the gush of a chatterbox. Charlotte is further ridiculed for her obsessions about housekeeping and food. In these respects she is offered to us as an amusing butt. Elsewhere,

[1] *Volume the Second*, p. 74.

however, Jane Austen uses the girl as the point of view through which to analyse characters and events, in an observing function which is inconsistent with her other traits. When she is employed as commentator her style changes completely, becoming aphoristic and cold in tone. She can see through Lady Lesley, who 'plays, sings & Dances, but has no taste for either, and excells in none, tho' she says she is passionately fond of all'.[1] She strips the pretence of the 'violent partiality' which settled into

a downright Freindship, and ended in an established correspondence. She is probably by this time as tired of me, as I am of her; but as she is too polite and I am too civil to say so, our letters are still as frequent and affectionate as ever, and our Attachment as firm and sincere as when it first commenced.[2]

The satire, the shapeliness of expression, and the severity are Jane Austen's not Charlotte's.

Lady Lesley is a more convincing observer, a woman whose formidable personality is a combination of smartness and selfish bad temper, exhibited in comic self-dramatization. On first seeing the castle she reports to her friend:

It is actually perched upon a Rock to appearance so totally inaccessible, that I expected to have been pulled up by a rope; and sincerely repented having gratified my curiosity to behold my Daughters at the expence of being obliged to enter their prison in so dangerous & ridiculous a Manner.[3]

This sharpness is not confined to her private communications; it is equally marked in her behaviour, which precipitates the strains inherent in a second marriage—the problems of family jealousy, and conflicting interests over precedence and fortune.

The variegated and experimental nature of 'Lesley Castle' is evident in Letters 8 and 9. Except for the closing paragraphs of no. 9 these letters stand noticeably outside the comic mood. Eloisa's heart-broken appeal for sympathy and Mrs. Marlowe's kindly reply might almost be copied from Richardson's *Familiar Letters* (1741), models designed to guide correspondents in

[1] p. 88.   [2] p. 89.   [3] p. 95.

meeting the difficulties of public and private life. Eloisa hopes that the older woman will not think her 'girlishly romantic' in seeking a 'kind and compassionate Freind who might listen to my Sorrows without endeavouring to console me'.[1] The diction and thought of the letter verge upon sentimentalism, but the sentence movement is dignified, the girl's self-scrutiny honest, and her emotion bears no hint of exaggeration, indulgence, or literary falsification. In her reply Mrs. Marlowe is drawn as an exemplary wife and mother, a confidante who balances her concern for Eloisa with a sense of the responsibility she owes her husband and son. Richardson himself could not have done better in weighing these delicate issues.

However often in the past Jane Austen may have mocked the role of confidante, she valued it as an essential human relationship; it was a position she was one day to fill for her niece, Fanny Knight.[2] She probably intended that Letters 8 and 9, passages of true feeling, should serve as a foil to the various kinds of pretence and insincerity illustrated throughout the rest of the work, and analysed so amusingly in the last section of Mrs. Marlowe's letter. The contrast is simply made. The letters are an easy way of keeping apart the serious and comic areas, a separation which, for all its convenience, tends to weaken the structure. As yet her prose was not sufficiently flexible to reconcile varied tones of comedy and pathos.

'The three Sisters' escapes many of the weaknesses of 'Lesley Castle'. With its firm design and neatly-turned plot it reads like a short episode from a full-scale novel. Jane Austen now avoids lengthy passages of narrative or reported speech, and employs direct conversation. The effect is dramatic, and hits the tone of social comedy. Her subject—marriage for an establishment— was a crucial problem at this time, posing the question of expediency and idealism. Mary Stanhope, an eldest daughter, is fatherless, and without a dowry. In this situation marriage is an unromantic negotiation of settlements and rights, a bargaining

[1] pp. 112–13.   [2] Letters 103, 106.

treated here in unrestrained comedy. But the irony of the entertainment is as serious as Jane Austen's advice to Fanny Knight:
'Single Women have a dreadful propensity for being poor—
which is one very strong argument in favour of Matrimony.'[1]
On an earlier occasion she had written to the girl: 'Anything is
to be preferred or endured rather than marrying without Affection.'[2] The force of this argument is dramatized here.

The situation and characters are presented through the
letters of the two strongly contrasted girls, Mary and her
youngest sister, Georgiana. The elder girl is a fool, dazzled and
confused by the prospect of marriage. Her opening letter begins
on a note of naïve delight, and continues in a confusion of
hopes and fears. Georgiana writes clearly and wittily. Whereas
Mary, Marianne-like, calls Mr. Watts 'quite an old Man, about
two & thirty',[3] Georgiana speaks sardonically, in practical commendation:

> He is not more than two & thirty; a very proper age for a Man to
> marry at; He is rather plain to be sure, but then what is Beauty in
> a Man; if he has but a genteel figure & a sensible looking Face it is
> quite sufficient.[4]

The attitudes of the two sisters are further revealed in Georgiana's account of the dialogue and events which take place on
Mr. Watts's visit to settle the marriage terms. This vivid scene
is followed by another little comedy, the spectacle of Mary's
'triumph', the visit she pays to the Dutton girls, before whom
she preens herself in newly gained social consequence. The
direction of Jane Austen's art is clearly marked in these passages.
Her aim is to show how character is formed and defined in the
events of ordinary life, and how speech and behaviour are determined by a complex of personal and social considerations. But
this material required a less restrictive form, and in 'Catharine
or the Bower', the most important of the early works, there is
much freer treatment of these issues in direct narrative.

Before considering 'Catharine' it is convenient to examine

[1] *Letters*, p. 483.   [2] *Letters*, p. 410.
[3] *Volume the First*, p. 105.   [4] p. 112.

'Evelyn', preceding it in *Volume the Third* and probably composed close to the date given at the front of the notebook, 6 May 1792. An inscription inside the front cover refers to the contents of this manuscript as 'Effusions of Fancy by a very Young Lady Consisting of Tales in a Style entirely new',[1] a description that fits this work rather than 'Catharine', for 'Evelyn' is fanciful and original in every respect. It appears to stand outside the line of formal experiment we can trace in the other works of this period, belonging rather with 'Love and Friendship' and the 'History' as a critical work of art, embodying a response to certain literary fashions. The fanciful element is the fairy-tale perfection of the village and its inhabitants, and the hero's travels, parodying those of a romance-journey. The originality is the combination of this material with a satire upon current modes in the description of landscape and the Gothic setting.

Jane Austen's interest in landscape description was probably aroused by the practice of contemporary novelists, especially Mrs. Smith, whose elaborate set-pieces were much admired. Catherine Percival is conforming to this taste when she speaks so warmly of the descriptions of Grasmere in *Ethelinde*. Another writer to whom Jane Austen refers specifically in the juvenilia is William Gilpin, the topographer of the picturesque. In the *Biographical Notice* Henry remarked that her interest in his illustrated tours commenced 'at a very early age'.[2] Evidently she had read *The Highlands* (1789) by June 1790[3]; perhaps this was the basis for her little burlesque letter 'A Tour through Wales'.[4] The setting of Jane Austen's mature imaginative world is not, however, the picturesque or romantic scene, but the landscaped grounds, the vistas of the country house—an expression of eighteenth-century taste that reveals social character, which Jane Austen drew into the structure of her works.

In 'Evelyn' the setting is merely a literary joke that may have been suggested to her by Cowper's light satire in *The Task*.[5] The village is an idyllic spot 'in which neither Misery, Illhealth, or

[1] p. v.   [2] *Northanger Abbey*, p. 7.   [3] *Volume the Second*, note to p. 53.
[4] *Volume the Second*.   [5] i. 255–61, ii. 767–73.

Vice are ever wafted'.[1] The principal building, the home of the Webb family,

> was in the exact centre of a small circular paddock, which was enclosed by a regular paling, & bordered with a plantation of Lombardy poplars, & Spruce firs alternatively placed in three rows.[2]

The passage continues in this manner, with regular and meticulous enumeration, a satire upon the layout of the formal garden, by then outmoded, and also upon the elaboration of inconsequential detail.

To this is joined a satire on the background and atmosphere of the Gothic novel. In 1792 Jane Austen could regard it as just one more laughable variety of extravagant fiction, another kind of romance to be deflated. Gothic fiction had not then entered its phase of spectacular terror and excess. Of the works named in *Northanger Abbey* (some of which she would have found distasteful, as she was 'disgusted' at the 'indelicacies' of Madame de Genlis's *Alphonsine* (1806)[3]), none was published before 1793, and the Gothic strain in Horace Walpole, Clara Reeve, Sophia Lee, and Mrs. Radcliffe was relatively mild and inoffensive. When she mocks Gothic devices, incidentally in 'Lesley Castle'[4] and the 'History',[5] and more directly in 'Evelyn', there is none of the exasperation that sharpens her burlesque of sentimental fiction. Here, for example, Mr. Gower approaches the rugged grandeur of the castle in a gently critical vein, his taste refined by a year's stay at Evelyn:

> There was an irregularity in the fall of the ground, and a profusion of old Timber which appeared to him illsuited to the stile of the Castle, for it being a building of a very ancient date, he thought it required the Paddock of Evelyn lodge to form a Contrast, and enliven the structure. The gloomy appearance of the old Castle frowning on him as he followed it's winding approach, struck him with terror.[6]

Later, the scene of his departure ridicules the stock situation of a benighted traveller in a fearful place. Just as the satire is light and restrained, the story is likewise conducted on a level of

---

[1] p. 7.   [2] pp. 7–8.   [3] *Letters*, p. 173.
[4] *Volume the Second*, p. 95.   [5] Ibid., p. 135.   [6] pp. 19–20.

fantasy, wholly different from the farcical violence which marks the picaresque journeyings in 'Love and Friendship'.

Historically, this work is significant as Jane Austen's earliest joke upon Gothic fashions. It also reveals her capacity for precise visualization and exactitude of description, gifts which were to be developed in the later works, most significantly in *Mansfield Park*. The movements of the characters about the grounds of Sotherton, and the details of the setting, are closely related to the turn of future events, mirrored in the adventures of the party during that afternoon's visit. Ultimately, in *Sanditon*, the setting becomes an agent in the story, a considerable element in the meaning of the work. 'Evelyn' may have been a trifle thrown off to amuse the family but, no less than the obvious and ambitious experiments, it is a working out of certain ideas and methods which were to contribute to her design in the mature works.

If 'Evelyn' was something of a diversion, 'Catharine' is very different. For the first time, in attempt if not in achievement, we see the mark of an ambitious novelist. In scope and proportion the fragment is suited to be the opening of a full-scale work. The range and depth of the characterization, and the fullness of dialogue and action, are far in advance of anything she had attempted before, a progress that probably owed much to the example of Fanny Burney. There is a striking similarity in their subject-matter and themes, but a comparison with *Evelina* (1778) or *Cecilia* (1782) quickly confirms the distinction and originality of the younger writer.

'Catharine', like *Evelina*, might fittingly be sub-titled 'The History of a Young Lady's Entrance into the World'. Yet beside Fanny Burney's novels even this early undeveloped fragment serves to illustrate the point of George Moore's claim: 'Miss Austen was the inventor of the formula whereby domestic life may be described.'[1] Jane Austen's story moves quietly in the tempo of a country neighbourhood, where the most exciting events are the arrival of visitors and a ball. The characters are

[1] *Avowals* (1919), 1936, i. 34.

few and the incidents commonplace. By contrast, Fanny Burney's plots are adventure stories with an extensive social panorama, her action conventionally melodramatic, employing many devices typical of sentimental and Gothic fiction, with mysteries, mistaken identities, plotting villains, and comedy that turns to farce, often violent and cruel. Experience has little effect upon the heroines; our attention is concentrated upon their adventures, on the widely ranging scenes and the procession of humorous characters they encounter, not upon their response to this world. The articulation of this material is often faulty, the action episodic, interrupted by soliloquies and areas of didactic moralizing. As accounts of social life the two early novels are lively and entertaining; but from a wealth of material so varied and unorganized no coherent experience or meaning can emerge. Beside these works 'Catharine' can be said to tend 'towards the vase rather than the wash-tub';[1] the narrative is conducted with economy and concentration and the principal episodes developed with due regard to their place in the structure of the plot. Jane Austen maintained that she would never write outside the bounds of her experience;[2] she also insisted upon truth of representation. 'Catharine' is the first artistic statement of these principles, which were self-imposed. They owe nothing to the example of Fanny Burney, whose works are in the nature of romance compared with Jane Austen's sober fidelity. This is not to say, of course, that 'Catharine' is without fault. It was left unfinished, not, I believe, because Jane Austen lost interest, but because she recognized her failure with the heroine, and in this experiment the failure is remarkably instructive.

At the opening and close of the story Catharine is gently mocked as a sentimental figure, whereas in contact with Camilla Stanley she is drawn as a lively young woman of keen intelligence and wit, while in many of her dealings with Edward Stanley she is an *ingénue* of foolish simplicity. These three

---

[1] George Moore's figure to describe the shaping influence of Jane Austen's form upon the English novel (*Avowals*, p. 35).   [2] See below, p. 81.

aspects are not related to a growth in experience, nor do they compose a single, unified personality. A feature of Jane Austen's development in the mature novels is the increasing delicacy with which she was able to maintain the critical relationship between 'the current of ordinary life' and *la belle nature*. In 'Catharine' there is conflict, not harmony, between these areas, a discordance which centres on the heroine, whose realism and individuality are not consistent with the mocking resemblance she bears to the types of popular fiction.

At the opening Catharine is presented in a mildly sentimental colouring, whereas the circumstances and characters around her are realistic. Thus for the first few pages there is no certain indication whether or not the story is a burlesque. It begins (in the way of *Northanger Abbey*):

> Catharine had the misfortune, as many heroines have had before her, of losing her Parents when she was very young, and of being brought up under the care of a Maiden Aunt. . . .[1]

This is the typical situation of the distressed heroine. Accordingly, she has a sentimental retreat, the 'bower' of the title, which affords her 'constant releif in all her misfortunes'.[2] The circumstances of the Wynne girls belong to a harsher order of reality. Against her will the elder had been sent to find a fortune in Bengal, where she remained, 'Splendidly, yet unhappily married.'[3] The other was also unfortunately situated, a friendless, paid companion in a noble family. The dilemma of the impoverished orphan is a recurrent topic in Jane Austen, a poignant example of the economic and social vulnerability of women in the eighteenth century. At this point the literary satire aimed at Catharine is linked rather uncomfortably with social criticism declared in serious terms.

In conversation with Camilla she displays judgement and wit, quickly penetrating the other girl's parade of elegance and taste. She recognizes that Camilla uses words carelessly, as mere counters, without any genuine force of emotion or meaning.

[1] p. 31.   [2] p. 32.   [3] p. 35.

In time Catharine grows sufficiently assured to deflate this meaningless small-talk. She also displays verbal acuteness in her encounters with Edward, and in meeting the reproaches of her aunt. In this respect Catharine is a completely new type of heroine, the woman of spirit and intelligence, Jane Austen's distinctive tradition, continued in Elinor Dashwood and Elizabeth Bennet.

The heroine's worldly education is extended by Edward, a bumptious and persuasive man-of-fashion, the conventional rake-villain now modified to the scheme of polite domestic comedy. Very soon judgement deserts her. She is turned into a Marianne, an impressionable girl 'whose imagination was lively, and whose Disposition romantic'.[1] She fails to see that Edward is a trifler and that his flattering attentions are nothing but a diversion to pass the time and alarm her aunt, until, for a moment, she manages to escape her romantic delusion. Yet these sobering reflections give way before the charm of his 'animated & insinuating'[2] manner, and the internal conflict between 'sense' and 'sensibility' is continued until the final soliloquy, when she speculates melodramatically on Edward's departure from Chetwynde. Once again she assumes the role of sentimental heroine.

On the other hand (allowing for Jane Austen's modest aim in the portrayal of flat and static figures who undergo no change), Camilla, Edward, and Mrs. Percival are successful creations. Camilla represents the type of fashionable young lady whose education has fitted her for nothing but the display of accomplishments. She is an ignorant chatterer with a sophistication as shallow as her knowledge of history and literature. There is a serious and disapproving analysis of her deficient education, a subject which Jane Austen felt as strongly about as she was concerned for the predicament of the Wynne girls. The 'Maiden Aunt', Mrs. Percival, is another type, the comic chaperone now adapted by Jane Austen to her own purpose. Conventionally, she is plagued by a 'jealous Caution',[3] the 'constant apprehension'

[1] p. 106.   [2] p. 116.   [3] p. 31.

of her charge marrying 'imprudently'.[1] She is also a hypochondriac, with a further grand obsession 'that the whole race of
Mankind were degenerating'.[2] A figure of fun, she has, none
the less, an important place in the scale of values presented
through the characters and action. She shows up the affecta-
tions of Mrs. Stanley. At heart she is a woman of kindness and
common sense, not altogether unlike Mrs. Jennings, who at
first appears to be nothing more than a vulgar and inquisitive
match-maker, an embarrassment to the Dashwood sisters in
London and a particular torment to Marianne, yet who turns
out to be a woman of genuine loyalty and good nature. Perhaps
Mrs. Percival was destined to take a similar role for Catharine.
But the most we see of the Aunt is in her clash with Edward.
In this collision of neurotic prudence and devilment Catharine
is the innocent victim. The situation was ripe for development.
However, Jane Austen was not ready to translate farce into high
comedy; nor was she able to make this sphere of violent external
action a shaping element in the heroine's experience—as we see,
for example, in the most effective episode of the story, Catharine's arrival with Edward at the ball. Mrs. Percival's discomfi-
ture and consternation are brilliantly drawn, yet we learn little
about Catharine. There is no significant relationship between
character and action. Marianne Dashwood also offends social
propriety. But her transgressions, unlike those of Catharine,
are not so much accident, or the result of ignorance and in-
experience, as an aspect of her impetuosity, the rebelliousness
of a passionate, headstrong nature. Her behaviour is much more
deeply grounded in character, much more its expression, and is,
moreover, related to the theme of the work.

Jane Austen left 'Catharine' unfinished, perhaps because she
realized the weakness in her drawing of the heroine. She may
also have been dissatisfied with the style of the narrative, which
is very far from the ideal manner of social comedy, 'light, and
bright, and sparkling', with 'the playfulness and epigrammatism
of the general style'[3] (to use her own description of *Pride and*

[1] p. 38.   [2] p. 47.   [3] *Letters*, pp. 299, 300.

Prejudice). Much of the dialogue, which occupies nearly half the work, is crisply handled, the individual mannerisms nicely differentiated. Outside the areas of speech, however, the prose often lapses into an elegant and formal periodic manner, satisfying and polished after its fashion, but somehow distanced, and anonymous, precluding the shifts of tone and emphasis, the expressive control essential to the play of irony and satire. This heaviness in the writing is particularly noticeable in the account of Cecilia Wynne's Indian marriage. Jane Austen's aunt Philadelphia had been subjected to the same experience. We know from Jane Austen's letters and other works how strongly she felt about marriage without love. Yet the force of what must have been a personal emotion is not communicated. Her attitudes seem to have been muffled or displaced by an irrelevant concern for stylishness:

The eldest daughter had been obliged to accept the offer of one of her cousins to equip her for the East Indies, and tho' infinitely against her inclinations had been necessitated to embrace the only possibility that was offered to her, of a Maintenance; Yet it was *one*, so opposite to all her ideas of Propriety, so contrary to her Wishes, so repugnant to her feelings, that she would almost have preferred Servitude to it, had Choice been allowed her—. Her personal Attractions had gained her a husband as soon as she had arrived at Bengal, and she had now been married nearly a twelve-month. Splendidly, yet unhappily married.[1]

Only the last words remind us that the writer is Jane Austen.

The opposition between passion and reason is a recurrent theme in Jane Austen's writing—implicit in the earliest of the juvenilia, more clearly defined in 'Lesley Castle' and 'The three Sisters', drawn unsuccessfully in Catharine, and successfully in *Sense and Sensibility*. In 1792 her attitude was sometimes hard, with the simplicity and impatience of youth. As Miss Lascelles has observed, 'in romantic notions, aptitude for friendship, appetite for pleasure, and readiness to be pleased',[2] Catharine anticipates the heroine of *Northanger Abbey*.

[1] pp. 34–35.   [2] *Review of English Studies*, N.S., iii (1952), 184.

Yet there are differences. Catherine Morland is seen with the sympathy and tolerance of a grown woman, whereas Catharine Percival is presented, less patiently, through the candid gaze of a girl her own age, the vision sharp, satirical, and sometimes mocking.

3

LADY SUSAN AND
THE LOST ORIGINALS 1795–1800

BETWEEN 1793 and 1800 Jane Austen composed *Lady Susan* and the first versions of *Sense and Sensibility*, *Pride and Prejudice*, and *Northanger Abbey*. Unfortunately, so little of this writing has survived in its original form that the exact nature of her development over these years is uncertain. All that remains is a transcript of *Lady Susan* made some time later, and the merest scrap from the title-page of an early version of *Northanger Abbey*.[1] In the absence of manuscript evidence we have to rely upon the family records for information about the original versions of the three novels which underwent considerable change before publication. In the second part of this chapter I review what is known of these early works, and attempt a reconstruction of their chronology and general characteristics, a speculation which I hope is reasonable and justified, for without some working theory the course of Jane Austen's progress between *Lady Susan* (*c.* 1793/4) and *The Watsons* (1804–5) is left unduly obscure.

(1)

The manuscript of *Lady Susan* is an undated and untitled fair copy, almost free from correction and revision. Two of the leaves are watermarked 1805, and Dr. Chapman judges that

---

[1] It reads: 'Susan, A Novel in Two Volumes' (see description in the *Ninth Report of the Director of the Pierpont Morgan Library* (1958–9), p. 84). Dr. Cahoon, the Curator of Autograph Manuscripts, has dated it *c.* 1803, following *Facts and Problems*, p. 44, but he informs me that it could be earlier.

the work was composed and transcribed about this time. He develops this view in *Facts and Problems*, observing that Jane Austen's handling of the story is 'very unlike a novice'.[1] This is a dating much later than that given in the standard biographies. In the 1871 *Memoir* J. E. Austen-Leigh admitted that he was 'not able to ascertain when it was composed', but he deferred to the family tradition that it was 'an early production'.[2] According to the *Life* it was written in the same period as *Elinor and Marianne*, that is about 1795. This dating seems to be pure guess-work, an association of the two stories because both are in letters. Yet the evidence of the work itself supports this date. The style, structure, and characterization indicate early composition, close to 'Catharine', to which it stands in the same relationship as 'Catharine' holds to the earlier juvenilia, as an exercise in correcting technical and stylistic faults. *Lady Susan* has the evenness of tone and unity of style of which 'Catharine' stood most in need. Having there conducted her first considerable experiment in direct narrative, and failed, Jane Austen now returns to the less demanding form of the correspondence novel. She pays regard, as never before, to verisimilitude in the length, frequency, and contents of the letters. But perhaps growing tired of the plot, and finding its complications awkward to handle, she abandoned the letters and rounded off the story, disposing of the characters and completing the action summarily. In the 'Conclusion' she makes fun of the letter device which up to this point had been handled so effectively. This final section cannot have been added long afterwards, for the style has something of the stiffness we find in 'Catharine'; and there is nothing in the 'Conclusion' which would argue for a date of composition much later than that we assign to the body of the work. As I try to show in part ii, the course of Jane Austen's development from 1793 to 1805 is away from the letter, which she discarded in favour of direct narrative. To suggest, with Dr. Chapman, that this work was composed *c*. 1805 would be to assume a sudden and uncharac-

[1] p. 52.   [2] p. 201.

teristic regression, and whatever other date we assign, it is difficult to place *Lady Susan* in the same period as *The Watsons*, to which it is so inferior in conception and achievement.

Nevertheless, certain features of *Lady Susan* might well lead us to suppose it a work of some maturity. It displays the author's skill in the adaptation of stock themes and characters to an original design. We come across the types and situations which abound in eighteenth-century novels and comedies: the sophisticated and charming flirt, the tyrannical mother, the daughter to be sacrificed in a profitable marriage, the proud young man tempted and deceived by the adventuress, the family concern for his possible disgrace, the 'correct' and decorous ending, with the villainess unmasked, the young man wiser for his experience and rewarded with the girl he has saved. The fashionable world of Lady Susan, Mrs. Johnson, and Sir James Martin, with its Town values and dissipation, is worsted by the integrity and principle of family life in the country. Nothing here is new. Sentimental fiction is full of tyrannical parents, persecuted children, and forced marriages, already parodied by Jane Austen in the conflict between Sir Reginald and his son in 'Love and Friendship'. Conventionally, these situations would lead to violence and melodrama, as indeed they do in Jane Austen's hands. But the violence is in the disruption of personal and family relationships, not in action; and the melodrama is in the character of Lady Susan, in the clash between her desperate concern for reputation, for social propriety and acceptance, and the need to indulge her aggressive personality.

There is no precedent for a short epistolary novel largely designed to exhibit this type of character. Neither did Jane Austen have any model for the distinctive surface quality of the writing, which Dr. Chapman has defined so accurately as 'the hard polish of the style' creating 'a vivid illusion'.[1] Although the letters cover a wide range—from the formal gravity of the Richardsonian conduct epistle (no. 12, Sir Reginald to his son) to the emotion of Frederica's desperate appeal to Reginald

[1] *Facts and Problems*, p. 52.

(no. 21)—the main correspondence, of Lady Susan, Mrs. Johnson, Mrs. Vernon, and Reginald, has a common fluency and precision of manner, a sharpness of outlook, which gives the work as a whole such a pronounced surface. Equally striking is the seriousness of tone, so remote from the comedy and ironic play of the juvenilia and the novels. Only in the 'Conclusion' and the three letters between Lady Susan and Mrs. Johnson is there any departure from the prevailing mood. The strength of the dominant, non-ironic temper can be judged by the manuscript change of 'feelings' to 'Sensibilities',[1] a word which comes from the juvenilia heavy with burlesque overtones. The context exerts its own mood so strongly that these associations are completely eliminated.

It is clear, however, that what we chose to call its originality or maturity is won at the cost of a radical simplification in subject-matter and technique. Such concentration upon a central figure is an economy of purpose which involves economy of means. In comparison with 'Catharine' and many of the earlier pieces there is a marked absence of dramatic life and variety. Much of the dialogue and action is in reported form which lacks the immediate force of Jane Austen's finest social comedy. The minor figures exist only by virtue of their place in the heroine's scheming, as connivers, victims, or enemies. Mrs. Vernon and Mrs. Johnson have a long-standing connexion with Lady Susan, but they function in the work as points of view, not characters. At first Reginald promises to exert a shaping influence upon events. His opening letter (no. 4) seems to announce a young man of wit and spirit, a fit match for Lady Susan. But we are disappointed. He soon emerges as a colourless dupe, and by the end of the story he is little more than a self-righteous prig. Having drawn Lady Susan, Jane Austen seems to have lost interest in the other figures, and lets the work run to a conventional ending, without any serious regard to probability and distinction in character and action.

The qualities and limitations of the work are defined in the

[1] Note to p. 142, l. 18.

figure of Lady Susan. Alone of Jane Austen's central characters she is drawn without affection or sympathy, a woman totally unprincipled, an adulteress, a liar, a hypocrite, a mother without love for her child and intent only on self-gratification. Within these terms she is precisely and simply portrayed. The convincing and consistent study is of an unfeminine nature, predatory and aggressive, only to be satisfied in the domination of others, as we see in Letter 7, where she indulges her malicious delight at the prospect of conquering Reginald:

There is something about him that rather interests me, a sort of sauciness, of familiarity which I shall teach him to correct. . . . There is exquisite pleasure in subduing an insolent spirit, in making a person pre-determined to dislike, acknowledge one's superiority. I have disconcerted him already by my calm reserve; & it shall be my endeavour to humble the Pride of these self-important De Courcies still lower. . . .[1]

As an individual character-study Lady Susan is remarkable and fascinating, a figure who would not be out of place in the pages of Wycherley or Congreve.[2] But Jane Austen's main purpose was to examine what happens to such a person in polite society, in situations where her natural impulses conflict with the specific obligations of her age and position. How is Lady Susan to reconcile her assertive nature with the fact of her poverty, her widowhood, her notoriety as a vicious woman, and her present need to find acceptance in a household of high moral tone? While Lady Susan mocks 'that great word "Respectable" '[3] she also cherishes it as a social cachet, valuing her claim to respectability as much as success with Reginald. For fear of scandal she breaks her liaison with Manwaring, announcing with proud indignation that she will never become

---

[1] p. 27.
[2] J. A. Levine surveys what he calls the 'Merry Widow' figure of seventeenth and eighteenth-century literature ('Lady Susan: Jane Austen's Character of the Merry Widow', *Studies in English Literature 1500–1900*, i. 4 (1961), 23–34). Independently, and by very different routes, we reach the same conclusion—that the inspiration for this heroine came to Jane Austen from literature, not life.   [3] p. 6.

a party to those 'inexcusable' women 'who forget what is due to themselves & the opinion of the World'.[1] Towards the 'World' she turns a face of virtue whose restraint, plausibility, and persuasive strength are established in her dealings with Mrs. Vernon and Reginald.

The conflict between impulse and her regard for social prudence is revealed mainly through the account of motives and stratagems that she confides to Mrs. Johnson. The letters of Mrs. Vernon examine her from the opposite point of view, that of a keen, antagonistic observer who reports the progress of Reginald's infatuation to their anxious mother. Through these two sets of letters we follow the dramatic thread, the curve of Reginald's opinion, which measures the success of deception from a third point of view. Gradually Jane Austen secures a shaping tension through the juxtaposition of these strongly contrasted letters, all of which tell of the commanding personality of a brilliant hypocrite. On the other hand, the distinctive force of this study entails a drastic simplification of character. Lady Susan is built up (like the work itself) by the accumulation and fitting together of a series of limited and disparate observations. In the later novels Jane Austen evolved a mode of presentation which unites and reconciles the different points of view through the author's narrative, the total and mediating point of view that can divine relationships and comprehend meanings far beyond the range of epistolary fiction. In a unified and inclusive medium characters can be presented with a force of dramatic insight and realism unattainable in a fragmented treatment. Moreover, the judgements declared upon Lady Susan are rigid statements of approval or disapproval; none of the correspondents is capable of more. Not until the 'Conclusion' is there any relaxation of this serious and unsubtle mood. By then Jane Austen must have realized that neither the form nor the material of the study was adequate to embody the view of life, both sympathetic and ironic, in which her imagination could be most fully engaged.

[1] p. 64.

The family biographers (and, no doubt, many other readers) have been puzzled or disturbed by Jane Austen's close attention to a central figure more a villainess than heroine. The authors of the *Life* were surprised 'that an inexperienced girl should have had independence and boldness enough to draw at full length a woman of the type of Lady Susan', whom they describe as a 'wholly sinister figure'.[1] M. A. Austen-Leigh shares this rather naïve outlook on the nature of experience and inspiration, arguing that 'this remarkable analysis of a vicious woman's nature'[2] is taken directly from life, and suggesting an historical basis for the characters and situation. I discuss this theory in the Appendix, but it should be said at once that such an interpretation cannot be justified on literary grounds. In the first place the family biographies take an exaggerated view of the heroine. One would say that it is Jane Austen's very failure to make Lady Susan a figure of real menace that asserts the author's essential ignorance of a 'wholly sinister' or 'vicious' woman. Secondly, as far as we can judge, *Lady Susan* is free from the obvious family allusions so important in the juvenilia. It reads as an autonomous and complete creation. The aesthetic distance between the author and her subject is strictly preserved. Nothing within the work invites us to speculate about its origins.

If we are to look outside *Lady Susan* it is not to search for sources or causal factors in its writing, but to note its relationship with Jane Austen's other works, particularly in respect of its heroine. Lady Susan's flirtatiousness and the powers of 'Intellect and Manner'[3] are single aspects of character treated in many of the important figures of the later novels. Flirts, both men and women, are the villains of Jane Austen's world, and deception in love, either suffered personally or observed in others, is a major enlargement of the heroine's experience. Progress towards self-knowledge involves the heroine's contact with the heartless or thoughtless—Edward Stanley, Isabella Thorpe, Wickham, Willoughby, Frank Churchill, and the Crawfords. It is not Elizabeth Bennet's 'prejudice', I am sure, that wholly

[1] p. 81.   [2] *Personal Aspects*, p. 100.   [3] p. 36.

explains the severity of her attitude towards Lydia;[1] and the direction of the creator's judgement is again felt in Emma Woodhouse's passionate censure of Frank Churchill.[2] Lady Susan personifies deception in its ugliest form; and Jane Austen's disapproval is without pity. Through this work she was able to relieve the pressure of her distaste; whereas, in the mature novels, she draws upon this feeling creatively—the deceivers are dangerous because they threaten people more important to us than Reginald and Frederica, and more human because they are treated with wit and sympathy.

The other prominent aspect of Lady Susan's character is her strength of mind and brilliance of manner, qualities which relate her on one side to the society woman, Lady Susan Lesley, of 'Lesley Castle', and more positively to the new heroine of the 1780's and 1790's, the girl whom Jane Austen and her sister-novelists were turning into a sufficient and independent figure, born to a higher destiny than sentimental romance. Before Lady Susan there was Catharine Percival, a spirited and witty young woman; afterwards this line is continued in Elinor Dashwood, Elizabeth Bennet, and Emma Woodhouse. Lady Susan has many accomplishments; but Jane Austen believed that rank, intellect, brilliance, education or breeding are nothing without principles and moral sense, a conviction which underlies her judgement here, as in all the later works.

(11)

The most important source of information about the lost manuscripts is a memorandum by Cassandra giving the dates of composition and a few words of description. Unfortunately, until the note was reproduced in 1954[3] the only available text was a version quoted incorrectly and incompletely in the *Life*,[4] and hitherto all time-tables of writing have incorporated the errors and omissions of this family source. I present the note in full, as its precise details are essential to a review of the lost

---

[1] *Pride and Prejudice*, p. 231.
[2] *Emma*, pp. 396–7.
[3] *Minor Works*, facing p. 242.
[4] pp. 80, 96–97.

originals (moreover, as Dr. Chapman makes no reference to the discrepancies, his chronologies remain uncorrected).

First Impressions begun in Oct 1796 Finished in Augt 1797. Published afterwards, with alterations & contractions under the Title of Pride & Prejudice. Sense & Sensibility begun Nov. 1797 I am sure that something of the same story & characters had been written earlier & called Elinor & Marianne Mansfield Park, begun somewhere about Feby 1811—Finished soon after June 1813 Emma begun Jany 21st 1814, finished March 29th 1815 Persuasion begun Augt 8th 1815 finished Augt 6th 1816

North-hanger Abbey was written about the years 98 & 99

C.E.A.

The provenance of this note is unknown, but there is strong evidence for its date and authority (which has been questioned).[1] Some of the details appear to have been copied from Jane Austen's personal record of the composition of *Mansfield Park*, *Emma*, and *Persuasion*.[2] The wording of the two notes is identical; the arrangement differs slightly, the entries for the last two novels being in reverse order. From the phrasing of Cassandra's entries for the other works it appears that she was relying on memory, a first-hand recollection of her sister at work. A niece overheard Jane Austen reading the original version of *Pride and Prejudice* to Cassandra while 'the composition of the story was still a secret kept from the knowledge of the elders';[3] presumably Cassandra's first acquaintance with the other novels was made in the same way. The final reference on the note, to 'North-hanger Abbey', shows that the entry was made after March 1817, for Jane Austen was then referring to her story as 'Catherine'.[4] The slightly eccentric spelling (perhaps indicating a Hampshire pronunciation) leads me to believe that Cassandra noted the title before the book was published in December 1818, otherwise it is unlikely that she would have given it this irregular

[1] C. S. Emden, '*Northanger Abbey* Redated?', *Notes and Queries*, cxcv (1950), 407–10.   [2] Reproduced in *Plan of a Novel*, p. 36.   [3] *Life*, p. 73.   [4] *Letters*, p. 484.

form. If the note was written between March 1817 and December 1818, the most probable date within this period would be soon after her sister's death, in July 1817, when Cassandra may have recorded these details for the benefit of the family.

The memorandum appears to have been the source for the information given in the 1870 *Memoir*, where *First Impressions* and *Sense and Sensibility* are correctly dated, and the wording of the entry for *Elinor and Marianne* is closely followed. A major discrepancy concerns *Northanger Abbey*, said to have been 'certainly first composed in 1798',[1] and completed the same year.[2] The *Life* correctly dates *First Impressions* and *Sense and Sensibility*; but *Northanger Abbey* is now said to have been written in 1797 and 1798, and without warning some of the other details are omitted. According to this unlikely chronology Jane Austen would have been occupied with *Northanger Abbey* at the same time as in turn she was writing *First Impressions* and turning *Elinor and Marianne* into *Sense and Sensibility*. The memorandum indicates what surely must be the real case, that she was writing these novels successively, in the order *First Impressions*, *Sense and Sensibility*, and *Northanger Abbey*, between October 1796 and 1799. With this time-table we can begin to reconstruct the stages in Jane Austen's choice between epistolary and narrative form, and make some tentative suggestions about the characteristics of these early novels.

Even though Jane Austen abandoned the letters before completing *Lady Susan*, her first serious attempt at a correspondence novel, at least she was prepared to cast her next work in the same form. According to the *Life*[3] *Elinor and Marianne* was an epistolary novel, written and read to the family before 1796. Two of these facts are corroborated in a note by Caroline Austen: 'Memory is treacherous, but I cannot be mistaken in saying that Sense and Sensibility was *first* written in letters, and *so* read to her family.'[4] In November 1797 Jane Austen began

---

[1] p. 63.   [2] p. 198.   [3] p. 80.
[4] Quoted by Dr. Chapman, *Facts and Problems*, p. 42. As Caroline was born in 1805 she must have picked up these details from family talk.

a drastic revision, abandoning the letters for the design we now find in *Sense and Sensibility*, giving the work, as the 1870 *Memoir* says, 'its present form'.[1] The change affected structure rather than content; comparing *Sense and Sensibility* with the earlier version Cassandra wrote that it was 'something of the same story & characters'.[2] Twelve years later came the revision of 1809–10 at Chawton, presumably the last before Jane Austen corrected the proofs in 1811 prior to publication in November of that year.

The apprentice quality of *Elinor and Marianne* can be surmised from the fact that whereas Mr. Austen wrote to Cadell about terms of publication for *First Impressions*, only three months after its completion, no such inquiries were made on behalf of the earlier work. The name title suggests that the purpose of the letters was to effect a contrast simply between the two girls, one of sentimental cast, the other with powers of judgement, their differences of temperament being exhibited through the style of their letters and their point of view. This would continue and refine the type of brief and exaggerated comparison made between Margaret and Georgiana in 'The three Sisters', and among some of the correspondents in 'Lesley Castle' and the 'Collection of Letters'. It is not difficult to reconstruct a possible scheme of letters to this design. In *Sense and Sensibility* the narrative point of view accompanies Elinor for much of the work and she is frequently used as the means of introducing the author's commentary. In the original we can suppose that her letters also carried much of the story, probably to a friend of her own age at Norland. The existence of such a companion is hinted at in chapter 11, where we learn of Elinor's disquiet at the behaviour of Marianne and Willoughby:

> Her heart was not so much at ease, nor her satisfaction in their amusements so pure. They afforded her no companion that could make amends for what she had left behind, nor that could teach her to think of Norland with less regret than ever. Neither Lady Middleton nor Mrs. Jennings could supply to her the conversation she missed.[3]

[1] p. 63.   [2] See above, p. 53.   [3] p. 54.

'The conversation she missed' was not that of her mother and sisters, certainly not that of Mr. and Mrs. John Dashwood. Nothing inside the novel explains this reference. Probably it survives from the original correspondence scheme, where such a confidante would be required. Even when Elinor is away from Devon the bulk of the story would still be told in letters to the confidante rather than to Mrs. Dashwood and Margaret at Barton, for like Marianne they are sentimentalists, unsuitable to receive Elinor's serious reflections upon her sister's behaviour and the problems of her own situation. Jane Austen may have borrowed Elinor's analysis and judgement of Willoughby[1] from this part of the correspondence.

In other, more important respects, however, Jane Austen took great care to present the later Elinor as a character who belongs to this new form. By temperament and circumstance she is not an epistolary heroine. To Lucy Steele she has made a promise of silence; and it would go against the grain for a nature of such independence and integrity to pass on her fears and doubts about other people, even to a confidante. In the final version of *Sense and Sensibility* it is the very fact that Elinor has alone to bear her grief and her sister's troubles that makes her situation so poignant and renders her stoic behaviour an example to Marianne.

A number of Marianne's speeches read like passages from the letters of a sentimental heroine, as for example her impassioned soliloquy on leaving Norland,[2] her eulogy upon fallen leaves,[3] and, towards the end of the book, her hysterical outburst of self-accusation and gratitude.[4] These passages may have been carried over from her original letters to a confidante at Norland, a girl of matching temperament. The weakness of the structure and writing is also noticeable when Jane Austen uses the conventional patterns of sentimental and romantic melodrama, notably in the Willoughby–Marianne betrayal and the Colonel Brandon–Eliza–Willoughby sub-plot, episodes sketchily treated.

[1] p. 331.   [2] p. 27.   [3] pp. 87–88.   [4] pp. 345–6.

The change of title, probably at the time of the 1797 revision, signifies an important shift of emphasis. Although the sister-heroines still remain at the centre, it appears that the theme of the work was made much more explicit. In *Sense and Sensibility* many of the subordinate figures exhibit some positive or negative aspect of the qualities named in the title, and so assist in the definition of the heroines. The structural coherence of the work partly depends upon the effectiveness with which the ethical theme is dramatized through the incidents and characters. In this light the revision of 1797 can be seen as a change in form which enabled Jane Austen to lay a further pattern of meaning, establishing new relationships, and so reinforcing and unifying the significance of the characters, action, and theme.

As we have already seen, this transformation was not perfectly achieved. At times Jane Austen seems to have had difficulty in freeing herself from the original design. Throughout the work there is a hint of contrivance in the arrangement of the characters in antithetical groups and in the symmetry of the action, a stiffness that may be a legacy from the first draft. The opening chapter was probably written as a functional commencement to the new version. So undramatic beside chapter 2, or the beginning of *Pride and Prejudice*, it offers a rather bald sketch of the family situation and established the sisters' characters as precisely as they would be declared by their style and point of view in the first letters of a correspondence novel. By contrast the reader is kept in ignorance of Willoughby's character and intentions; the revelation is gradual, as it would have been in the epistolary novel, where the reader's understanding of him would be reached equally slowly through the girls' correspondence. Thus the influence of the original design can still be detected in *Sense and Sensibility*, not only in passages that seem to have found their way through from the first version, but also in some of the devices of narration and design that Jane Austen has adopted in order to refashion and incorporate epistolary material.[1]

[1] Miss Lascelles considers these questions in the Introduction to the new Everyman edition of *Sense and Sensibility* (1962).

Soon after the completion of *Elinor and Marianne* Jane
Austen began *First Impressions*, written between October 1796
and August 1797. It has been assumed that this was her first
major essay in direct narrative, and that three months after
its completion she went on to reconstruct *Elinor and Marianne*
in the light of this successful change. Certainly, there is no
evidence to the contrary, and we might expect some remark
in the family biographies (as we have for *Elinor and Marianne*)
had *First Impressions* been an epistolary novel. I believe, nevertheless, that there are grounds for considering whether it too
may not have been a novel in letters. In November 1797, three
months after its completion, Mr. Austen wrote to Cadell, inquiring about publication, describing the work as 'a manuscript
novel, comprising 3 vols., about the length of Miss Burney's
Evelina'.[1] *Evelina* was very popular, having then run to at least
nine editions since its appearance in 1778. It could be argued
that the comparison is merely one of length, and that this title
came naturally to Mr. Austen's mind as that of a best-seller. On
the other hand if the comparison has any further significance
it indicates a *First Impressions* very different from the extant
version. Not only is *Evelina* a third as long again as *Pride and
Prejudice*, but it is an epistolary novel. Could it have been that
the revisions of 1809–10, 1811, and 1812, were to reduce the
bulk of a letter novel to the more economical method of direct
narrative? In January 1813 Jane Austen wrote to Cassandra,
'I have lop't and crop't so successfully, however, that I imagine
it must be rather shorter than S. & S. altogether.'[2] This remark
is confirmed by Cassandra's note that *First Impressions* was
later published 'with alterations and contractions'. Dr. Chapman argues that in the last revision the 1811–12 calendar was
used for the time-scheme, and that the book as we know it 'was
not merely rewritten, but very largely recast'.[3] Such considerations lead me to raise the possibility that *First Impressions* was,

[1] *Life*, p. 97.
[3] *Letters*, p. 298. In fact, they are almost the same length.
[3] *Facts and Problems*, p. 79.

like *Elinor and Marianne*, a novel in letters, and that Jane Austen did not abandon this method until she began the revision of *Elinor and Marianne* three months later, in November 1797. If by that time she already had behind her the experience of writing one novel entirely in direct narrative, it is unlikely that so many traces of the original version of *Sense and Sensibility* would have found their way through to the second draft. *Sense and Sensibility* does not seem to have been written in the light of such technical practice; in too many respects it reads like a first venture in this form.

Just as *Elinor and Marianne* almost certainly contained a large element of burlesque directed at the sentimental heroine, so *First Impressions* may also have begun as a literary satire, although little remains in *Pride and Prejudice* to indicate such an origin. The object of the burlesque is hinted at in the title, for the phrase 'first impressions' comes directly from the terminology of sentimental literature, and Jane Austen would certainly have met it in *Sir Charles Grandison*, where its connotations are briefly defined.[1] She would have known a more recent usage in *The Mysteries of Udolpho* (1794), where the heroine is told that by resisting first impressions she will 'acquire that steady dignity of mind, that can alone counterbalance the passions'.[2] Here, as commonly in popular fiction, 'first impressions' exhibit the strength and truth of the heart's immediate and intuitive response, usually love at first sight. Jane Austen had already attacked this concept of feeling in 'Love and Friendship', and in *Sense and Sensibility* it is a deeply-founded trait of Marianne's temperament: 'She expected from other people the same opinions and feelings as her own, and she judged of their motives by the immediate effect of their actions on herself',[3] a doctrine which she tries to justify to Elinor.[4] There is a striking reversal of this concept in *Pride and Prejudice*; first impressions are effective with Elizabeth Bennet, yet in circumstances altogether unsentimental. The

---

[1] See above, p. 11.   [2] i. 14.
[3] p. 202.   [4] pp. 58–59.

moment she catches sight of Darcy's family home she feels 'that to be mistress of Pemberley might be something!';[1] it is this sense of property which warms her heart towards Darcy, as she later admits to Jane,[2] jokingly, but speaking more truly than she knows, confessing to a worldliness, a common humanity which no sentimental heroine could possess. Elizabeth's other qualities—her intelligence, wit, and detachment—are also thoroughly anti-sentimental. Her violent first impressions of Darcy derive from prejudice and false reasoning; and he, in turn, is no romantic hero, no 'interesting' lover, but a taciturn, apparently unsociable fellow. From her initial meeting with him at the ball, and her encounters with Wickham, she has to learn how little the first impressions of her sharp intelligence are to be trusted. She comes to recognize how inadequate they are as a basis for judgement,[3] and this is further stressed in Jane Austen's commentary.[4]

The original title may have been discarded following the publication of a *First Impressions* by Mrs. Holford in 1801, and the second title could have been suggested by the closing pages of *Cecilia*, where the phrase 'pride and prejudice' is printed in capitals three times in a single paragraph, pointing the moral of the story.[5] In the revision of *Elinor and Marianne* the contraries sense and sensibility may have been extended to find expression throughout the book; so too in the re-working of *First Impressions* the pride of Darcy and the prejudice of Elizabeth may have been more subtly presented, as weaknesses common to both, and framed in a schematic relationship among the other characters. In the original letter form Elizabeth could have been the principal correspondent, writing to Charlotte Lucas and Mrs. Gardiner, while Darcy would have guardedly reported his side of events to other friends, including Bingley.

By the time *Northanger Abbey* was commenced in 1798 Jane Austen had written three works besides the juvenilia: *Lady*

---

[1] p. 245.   [2] p. 373.   [3] pp. 140–1.   [4] p. 279.
[5] v. 379–80. Dr. Chapman points to this and other possible connexions between the books, in his appendix to *Pride and Prejudice*, pp. 408–9.

Susan and *Elinor and Marianne* in letters, as also may have
been the third, *First Impressions*. Assuming that her decision to
employ direct narrative dates from the conversion of *Elinor and
Marianne* in November 1797, it is almost certain that from its
beginning *Northanger Abbey* was conceived in this form, though
in other respects the original must have differed slightly from
the text we have. The 'Advertisement, by the Authoress',
written about 1816/17, and prefaced to the first edition of 1818,
states that 'This little work was finished in the year 1803, and
intended for immediate publication.'[1] The work was then
known as *Susan*, and sold to the publisher Crosby in Spring
1803. In 1816 the manuscript was repurchased from Crosby,
and is next heard of on 13 March 1817, possibly just after the
'Advertisement' had been prepared. Jane Austen wrote to
Fanny Knight: 'Miss Catherine is put upon the Shelve for
the present, and I do not know that she will ever come out.'[2]
As in the case of the 1803 revision, that of 1817 has left almost
nothing to indicate the nature or extent of the changes: if we
trust the 'Advertisement' they were probably slight. Jane
Austen was in her last illness at that time, and was occupied
with *Sanditon* from January to 18 March. The only details that
must conclusively be additions to the original are the references
to Maria Edgeworth's *Belinda* (1801), and the alteration to the
heroine's name, some time between 1803 and 1817. The change
from the original title may have followed the publication of an
anonymous *Susan* in 1809.

This account of its textual history suggests that the extant
version of *Northanger Abbey* is close to its original form. Unlike
the other works it seems to have undergone no large-scale
structural alteration, and the burlesque note, which I believe
to have been strong in all three originals, is prominent here,
whereas it breaks through only occasionally in *Sense and Sensibility*, and is almost undetectable in *Pride and Prejudice*, except
in two places: Elizabeth's enraptured speech on receiving the
Gardiners' invitation to join them on a tour to the Lakes,[3] and

[1] p. 12.   [2] *Letters*, p. 484.   [3] p. 154.

the extract from Caroline Bingley's letter written, as Elizabeth comments, in 'high flown expressions'.[1] Otherwise the broader literary satire has become muted in revision. In *Northanger Abbey* the patterns of burlesque are elaborate and ingenious, but they are not always exactly related to the course of the heroine's experiences and adventures, and there is a good case for Mr. Emden's theory[2]: that Jane Austen added the Gothic element to a story which was originally concerned with a young girl's entry into society, not unlike the adventures of Catharine Percival.

There is no question that *Northanger Abbey* was ever an epistolary work. At one point the burlesque is directed specifically against the possibility of Catherine having either a correspondent or a confidante, and only nine letters are either mentioned or given in the narrative. By itself, this figure is of little value, but its relevance to the question of form becomes clear when we notice the prominence of letters (by reference or quotation) in the two other novels. In *Sense and Sensibility* twenty-one letters are mentioned, quoted, or given verbatim and in *Pride and Prejudice* no fewer than forty-four, including references to a 'regular and frequent'[3] correspondence between Elizabeth and Charlotte Lucas, and the further regular communications of Elizabeth and Jane with Mrs. Gardiner, a very credible system of letters to carry much of the story in an epistolary version. If this reconstruction is feasible it supports my theory that, like *Sense and Sensibility*, *Pride and Prejudice* was originally a novel-in-letters, and confirms the accepted view of *Northanger Abbey*, as having undergone no large-scale alteration after 1799.

[1] p. 116.   [2] See above, p. 53, note 1.   [3] p. 146.

4

THE WATSONS

(1)

THE twelve years between the completion of *Northanger Abbey* in 1799 and the commencement of *Mansfield Park* in 1811 are almost empty of original work, a remarkable contrast to the other, highly creative periods of Jane Austen's life. During these middle years there was only one new piece, *The Watsons*, of which no more than the opening section (about 17,500 words) was written before she abandoned the story in 1805. For a fourth novel the fragment is surprisingly undeveloped; probably Jane Austen's failure to continue the work later was in recognition of its serious flaws; perhaps, too, she felt out of sympathy with the almost unrelieved bleakness of the social picture, and the asperity of the satire. In these respects *The Watsons* stands apart from the other novels; it signals a failing in generosity and a loss of creative power which may be related to the circumstances of her life at this time.

In 1801, with her parents and sister, Jane Austen left Steventon. For the next eight years she lived in a succession of temporary homes, at London, Southampton and Bath, scenes of town life offering a wealth of observation. But as we learn from her letters, she was never completely happy away from a settled country home, with its domestic ties and affections, the surroundings in which she was best able to write, and which she found again at Chawton in 1809, when she at once took up the manuscripts of *Sense and Sensibility* and *Pride and Prejudice*, with publication in view.[1] In 1801 her circumstances were very different: the family audience was dispersed, and there was

[1] W. Austen-Leigh and M. G. Knight, *Chawton Manor and its Owners* (1911), p. 168.

no encouragement to her writing from outside. Already, in 1797, the publisher Cadell had refused to read the manuscript of *First Impressions*. A further disappointment was the failure of Crosby to bring out *Northanger Abbey*, which he had accepted in 1803 for immediate publication, advertising it that same year. Perhaps too, at a far deeper level, her imaginative powers may have been numbed by private sorrows. The story of her emotional relationships, of the attachments that might have reached marriage, is obscure and conflicting in detail.[1] Nevertheless, the weight of evidence suggests that between 1800 and 1803 her love was tragically ended. This experience, with the other discouragements, was not an immediate inspiration, as it might have been to other artists. Instead, it seems to have interfered with her creative powers, which were only restored on her return to the stability of family life that she found again at Chawton some years later.

The manuscript of *The Watsons* is an undated first draft, heavily corrected and revised. Following the evidence of the 1803 watermark Dr. Chapman places its composition in that year or soon after; another suggestion puts it as late as 1807–8.[2] In fact a more precise dating can be given. Fanny Lefroy (a granddaughter of James Austen) records that 'Somewhere in 1804 she began "The Watsons", but her father died early in 1805 [27 January] and it was never finished.'[3] In the previous month she had lost her dearest friend, Mrs. Lefroy,[4] and we can understand the pressure of circumstances that made it difficult to

---

[1] These matters are set out in *Facts and Problems*, ch. 5; and see my note 'Jane Austen: A Broken Romance?', *Notes and Queries*, ccvi (1961), 464–5.

[2] E. C. Brown, 'The Date of *The Watsons*', *Spectator*, 11 June 1927, pp. 1016–17.

[3] 'Is it Just?', *Temple Bar*, lxvii (1883), 277. Neither of the family biographies refers to these circumstances. Fanny Lefroy could have heard of them from her mother. Cassandra told the nephews and nieces of Jane Austen's plans for the story's continuation (1871 *Memoir*, p. 364), and she may then have mentioned the date it was abandoned.

[4] The fourth anniversary of her death, 16 December 1808, was Jane Austen's thirty-third birthday, when she wrote her longest, most serious and important poem, 'To the Memory of Mrs. Lefroy' (*Minor Works*, pp. 440–2, with two additional stanzas quoted in the *Spectator*, 29 February 1952, p. 257).

continue the story, which was, anyway, proceeding unsatis-
factorily.

The 1871 *Memoir* offers a wholly different explanation—
that Jane Austen put the work aside when she realized 'the evil
of having placed her heroine too low, in such a situation of
poverty and obscurity as, though not necessarily connected
with vulgarity, has a sad tendency to degenerate into it'.[1] But
this view derives from the social attitudes of the 1860's;[2] not
from Jane Austen, who uses the word 'vulgarity' as a judgement
against coarseness of behaviour and feeling, never as an index
of class or wealth. The circumstances of Jane Fairfax, Mrs.
Smith, and Fanny Price at Portsmouth are sufficient evidence
that she was quite prepared to treat subject-matter that moves
just as close to the level of poverty and unfashionable life endured by the Watsons. And far from any degeneration in her
position (that is, judged socially, in J. E. Austen-Leigh's terms),
Emma was to refuse a peer and marry a clergyman. If Jane
Austen faced any particular problem in the delineation of her
central figure it was literary, not social; she was telling the story
of a distressed heroine, the staple character of sentimental and
Gothic fiction. It is hardly surprising that at a first attempt she
should meet some difficulty in appropriating this subject to her
own kind of domestic comedy.

(II)

From the fragment and its proposed continuation the total
design is clear. The story turns on the sufferings and endurance
of a sensitive, educated girl, whose life is made almost un-
bearable by the impertinence and snobbery of her family and
neighbours. Further hardships are to be borne when she leaves
Stanton, until she eventually finds happiness in marriage. Jane
Austen was establishing the situation of the distressed heroine

---

[1] p. 296.
[2] Elsewhere Austen-Leigh displays a similar bias: in his remarks upon
her circle of acquaintances (p. 17), on Steventon Rectory (pp. 19–20) and
on the last three novels (pp. 145–6).

in a domestic setting, in 'the current of real life', with a considerable advance upon the degree of realism achieved by Fanny Burney. The leading adventures of Evelina and Cecilia take place in London society, a world far removed from that of romantic melodrama; none the less, these heroines are still idealized and the action remains melodramatic. Jane Austen treats this subject in a satirical comedy of daily life; where, for example, the arrival of a chance visitor when the family is dining at an unfashionable hour can provide the staple drama of character and action. The 'little social commonwealth'[1] of the family and neighbourhood is drawn with penetration and economy. Logan Pearsall Smith writes of Jane Austen's capacity to render 'the moral atmosphere of places, the tones, that is, of collective feeling, the moral climates which are produced by, and surround, different groups of people, as with a body of dense and saturated air, the places where they live'.[2] In *The Watsons* the 'moral atmosphere' has nothing of the rich density we find in *Mansfield Park* and the other late novels, yet a distinct social climate is established in the opening lines. Jane Austen's certainty of purpose and command of technique can be judged from the manuscript, where this account of D. and its neighbourhood (in the first paragraph of the story) is highly developed and almost free from correction and revision.

The first winter assembly in the Town of D. in Surry was to be held on Tuesday Octr ye 13th, & it was generally expected to be a very good one; a long list of Country Families was confidently run over as sure of attending, & sanguine hopes were entertained that the Osbornes themselves would be there. The Edwardes' invitation to the Watsons followed of course. The Edward's were people of fortune who lived in the Town & kept their coach; the Watsons inhabited a village about 3 miles distant, were poor & had no close carriage; & ever since there had been Balls in the place, the former were accustomed to invite the Latter to dress dine & sleep at their House, on every monthly return throughout the winter.[3]

---

[1] *Persuasion*, p. 43.
[2] 'Jane Austen' (1924), in *Reperusals and Re-Collections* (1936), p. 369.
[3] pp. 1–2.

The immediate function of the passage, to set the scene for Emma Watson's entry to this world, and to introduce the promise of action, is performed with economy and directness. It brings to our notice the ethos of the neighbourhood, alive to the assembly and responding to it with anticipation. The hope 'that the Osbornes *themselves* would be there' renders the bated breath of D. in a single word. Our attention is confined (as it is in the episodes which follow) not so much because wider concerns are excluded, as because the present context is projected so firmly.

The opening lines prepare us for the assembly, the heroine's first public appearance, where next to the Osbornes she is to be the centre of attention. As the action proceeds we see Emma moved from this exposed position into a smaller area, the bond of affection with Elizabeth. This uncertain calm is disturbed by the visit of Lord Osborne and Tom Musgrave, and shattered by the arrival of Margaret and Mr. and Mrs. Robert Watson. Gradually she is forced back into the closed world of her own reflections and memories. When the story breaks off the solitude of reading is her sole refuge from the painful awareness of her brother's and sisters' '. . . Hard-hearted prosperity, low-minded Conceit, & wrong-headed folly'.[1] The situations constructed round Emma are like a narrowing tunnel, along which she moves through fields of successively more intense experience.

This account of the work's structure needs qualification. The transitions between the nine major episodes fail to overcome a slightly awkward movement from scene to scene. There are passages where the dialogue needs to be lightened, where details of description and action require filling out, and occasionally the progress from paragraph to paragraph is somewhat clumsy, although the revisions show Jane Austen already providing links and bridge passages, tightening the structure and easing the narrative flow. Full-scale revision would have eliminated these and other relatively unimportant faults.

[1] p. 117.

The remaining and overriding difficulty would be that of making Emma a sufficient heroine: sensitive, intelligent, spirited, charitable, affectionate and high-principled, the possibilities for her development are limited. She is perceptive with others and has almost nothing to learn about herself. This judicious, almost static point of view is useful as the novelist's entry to the work, one of the means of interpreting people and events to the reader. In other of the novels, for example, Elinor Dashwood, Henry Tilney, and Mr. Knightley serve this end, as well as participating fully in the action. But they are not placed at the heart both of the action and of the experience of the work, as Emma Watson is. In *Sense and Sensibility* Elinor Dashwood occupies a central position, as the point of view mainly to observe Marianne; her own love-story is partly a foil to that of Willoughby and her sister. Like Henry Tilney and Mr. Knightley she is the external human agency assisting the heroine to see the truth about herself and other people. Our interest in Marianne, Catherine Morland and Emma Woodhouse is largely in watching them acquire, through their own mistakes and from the advice of others, maturity and wisdom to add to their own natural goodness, as yet undeveloped or misused. Emma Watson offers no such opportunities for shaping. She comes to Stanton fully armed with ideals; the vulgarity of her family can cause grief and pain, but her principles are not endangered. When she hears of Penelope's efforts to catch a husband she bristles with disapproval:

To be so bent on Marriage—to pursue a Man merely for the sake of situation—is a sort of thing that shocks me; I cannot understand it. Poverty is a great Evil, but to a woman of Education & feeling it ought not, it cannot be the greatest.[1]

Elizabeth warns her that when Penelope returns home she will laugh at these, the views of a 'rather refined'[2] sister. Emma replies, with justice and humility, 'If my opinions are wrong, I must correct them—if they are above my situation, I must endeavour to conceal them.'[2] Her reaction is admirable but

----

[1] pp. 9–10.   [2] p. 10.

colourless. In 1814 Jane Austen commented on a story by Anna
Austen: 'I wish you could make Mrs. F. talk more, but she
must be difficult to manage & make entertaining, because there
is so much good common sence & propriety about her that
nothing can be very *broad*',[1] an observation which applies equally
to her own presentation of Emma Watson.

There are, it is true, several occasions when Emma is brought
to life. She exhibits admirable spirit when Robert abuses her
Aunt Turner; and her remarks to Elizabeth are often touched
with a tone of mild irony. Her self-possession and wit are fully
dramatized during the unexpected call of Lord Osborne and
Tom Musgrave. Sensitive to the awkwardness of the occasion,
her humble surroundings, the condescension of the visit and
the unwelcome interest of the two young men, nevertheless she
is able to answer Lord Osborne's clumsy approaches with complete assurance, giving him a lesson in good manners. Her
behaviour is a model of how to administer a rebuke without
rudeness or loss of dignity. This is beautifully judged, the first
stage in the process (no doubt to be completed in the finished
work) or turning Lord Osborne into a gentleman and warming
his respect for the heroine. Yet while our admiration for Emma
grows, this scene fails to win sympathy for her. It is as if she is
too capable of dealing with a crucial situation, and she simply
displays the intelligence and verbal tact we already know her
to possess. At the assembly, however, an episode as finely
conceived as any in the mature novels, we are presented with
an attractive and lively heroine, a girl of immediate and charming generosity. In salving Charles's disappointment she 'did not
think, or reflect;—she felt & acted.'[2] Emma is fully engaged in
the situation and responding to it, her character seemingly
shaped or extended in the moment of action, its latent qualities
realized. But her presence in the rest of the work never approaches this level of spontaneous life, the plastic form of a
character in a sensitive and active relationship with people and

[1] Letter to Anna Austen, 9 September 1814 (*Letters*, p. 402).
[2] p. 41.

events. The deficiency of the heroine is particularly noticeable because the elements of her situation—the folly, vulgarity and malice of her family, and the values of the neighbourhood—are so vividly drawn. The imaginative life of the work is largely outside Emma Watson, who remains in low relief beside her brothers and sisters, and is quite overshadowed by Tom Musgrave, a figure who could hold his place alongside the most successful of Jane Austen's creations.

The account of the Watson family and their neighbours is the most severe and pessimistic view of society to be found in all Jane Austen's work. Personal integrity and family loyalties have given way to the snobberies of rank and riches, a struggle for status in which the Watsons are desperately and pitifully involved. Their predicament is exactly defined. The father, a poor and hypochondriac widowed clergyman, is quite unable to help his children and exercises no control over their fortunes or behaviour. Robert has escaped from poverty by marriage with his master's daughter, using her dowry to set himself up as an attorney. Sam is trying, rather forlornly, to win Miss Edwards, whose settlement makes her too good a match for a mere surgeon. The daughters are equally determined on marriage, Penelope ruthlessly and treacherously (she has already cheated Elizabeth of Purvis), Margaret fractiously and Elizabeth pitiably. For each of them marriage is the only way to avoid an impoverished old age.

Caught between the aristocratic patronage of Osborne Castle and the suburban gentility of Croydon, the Watsons ape the manners of both worlds. Thus Emma has to endure the condescension of Lord Osborne, the bustling impertinence of Tom Musgrave, the pretentious display of the Edwards; and from within the family there is the further pain of Robert's crude outspokenness, Margaret's affected tones of 'artificial Sensibility'[1] and Jane's 'familiar curiosity & Triumphant Compassion',[2] the hostile vulgarity of their manners so offensive to her, and so graphically depicted. Yet in this contrast Emma is a shadow.

[1] p. 92.   [2] p. 88.

Her response goes no further than a strong but simple embarrassment, shame, or disgust. There are very few occasions which demand fineness of discrimination or which imply a hidden depth to her nature. Only towards three people—Lord Osborne, her father, and Elizabeth—is she credited with attitudes more complex and flexible than simple approval or disapproval.

That Jane Austen could treat such a theme and figure successfully we know from *Mansfield Park*, where Fanny, a distressed and near-faultless heroine is (unlike Emma) endowed with life. The novel exhibits the interplay of experience and natural goodness (such as we see only once in *The Watsons*, at the assembly) by which a bewildered and often uncertain child develops into a young woman of just principles and moral taste. At eighteen Fanny realizes that

she had not yet gone through all the changes of opinion and sentiment, which the progress of time and variation of circumstances occasion in this world of changes. The vicissitudes of the human mind had not yet been exhausted by her.[1]

These 'changes of opinion and sentiment' are precisely what Emma is denied. Her outlook is formed at the opening of the story; her experiences cause pain without deepening her character or enlarging her understanding of life.

The second lesson that Jane Austen probably took from her failure with Emma (and which may have led her to success with Elinor Dashwood) is that the story should not rest so heavily upon the perceptive, observing heroine. For instance, in *Mansfield Park* we watch the captivation of Edmund by Mary Crawford largely through Fanny, and with her anxieties; and for part of the narrative she is used as the point of view to observe drama which involves her deeply, but in which she is not the principal actor. Later in *The Watsons* Jane Austen intended that 'much of the interest of the tale was to arise from Lady Osborne's love for Mr. Howard, and his counter affection

[1] p. 374.

for Emma, whom he was finally to marry.'[1] If the work had been continued on these lines she might then have returned to the beginning, to place Emma as an interested spectator rather than as a protagonist at the heart of the action.

(III)

Nothing in the manuscript suggests that Jane Austen had any radical second thoughts about the design or treatment. The alterations are mostly those of immediate correction and first revision, to refine detail and reinforce the verbal structure; and I think it can be assumed that these changes were made either at the time of writing, or very soon after the fragment was finished, before she had grown dissatisfied with the way the heroine was turning out. The opening lines are almost untouched. Presumably she realized her intention here satisfactorily, and many of the changes made later in the work emphasize qualities of style we can find at the beginning—order, clarity, definition, and economy of detail. For example, one widespread type of insertion strengthens the temporal or logical progression, giving a local continuity to incidents within the larger framework of times and dates. Under this head we find insertions such as *now, for now, just, then, thus, still, soon after, after a time, after a short pause, went on, in the present instance, at that moment.* In some places preterite forms of the verb have been changed to present participles, so assisting the continuative temporal movement, e.g. 'kindly undertook—chearfully undertaking, he had—having, had given—giving'. Many terms of emphasis and intensification are added: e.g. *particular, immediate, especially, more, very, very well, at least, even, actually, absolutely, never indeed, in fact;* and some of the alterations are in the same direction: e.g. 'no scruple—none of them the smallest scruple, a stiffer look than usual—her very stiffest look'. By these additions and changes the style is sharpened and the structure tightened.

Much the same process can be observed in passages where Jane Austen is eliminating material, retaining the significant

[1] 1871 *Memoir*, p. 364.

details, as in the description of the Edwards' house. We need only visualize a home which accords with their fortune and pretensions; references to its 'dull brick colour' and to the colour of the posts are profitably cancelled.[1] In the account of the assembly one sentence originally read:

It was always the pleasure of the company to have a little bustle & croud when they thus adjourned for what nine out of ten had no inclination . . .

The last line of the sentence is changed to 'for refreshment';[2] so Jane Austen controls a slightly indiscriminate play of wit, realizing that the slight irony could interfere with the larger purpose of keeping our attention on Emma's movements throughout the scene. The most interesting example of compression is in Elizabeth's account of her former admirer, Purvis. The original reads:

. . . I was very much attached to a young Man a neighbour—& he to me. Perhaps you may see him tonight. He is married Purvis & he has the Living of Alford about 14 miles off. We were very much attached to each other. . .[3]

This is reduced, perhaps because Jane Austen decided that Purvis was to figure less in the story. Some of the biographical detail is omitted, and the phrasing now more fully conveys Elizabeth's diffidence and embarrassment at mentioning him:

. . . I was very much attached to a young Man of the name of Purvis a particular friend of Robert's, who used to be with us a great deal. Every body thought it would have been a Match.[4]

Through other changes we can also watch Jane Austen searching for precision and expressive power in single words and phrases. For example, Emma refers to 'the scanty communication' that passed between herself and Elizabeth during her

---

[1] p. 19, note to l. 20. This is consistent with the advice to her niece Anna: 'your descriptions are often more minute than will be liked. You give too many particulars of right hand & left' (*Letters*, p. 401).
[2] p. 44, note to l. 16.   [3] p. 5, note to l. 6.   [4] p. 5.

fourteen years' absence from home; originally this read 'the scanty correspondence',[1] the noun implying the very sense of regularity that Jane Austen wished to avoid. When Charles is snubbed by Miss Osborne, Mrs. Blake's 'angry feelings' become a more ladylike 'mortification';[2] Margaret's 'querulous altercations' become 'querulous attacks';[3] this change extends the military metaphor at the opening of the sentence, and further emphasizes that Margaret confines her bad temper to Elizabeth and the maids, who do not answer back. At the close of the work Emma is said to have 'greater esteem' for Elizabeth; the original reading was 'greater affection',[4] but we know already that Emma loves her deeply and the new suggestion is that she is beginning to respect her on grounds other than those of sisterly emotion.[5] Other revisions are in the direction of increasing liveliness and colloquial vigour: the violin 'tuning' becomes 'Scrape';[6] 'unable to proceed' becomes 'hemmed in';[7] Robert Watson's glance at the mirror is changed from 'took a veiw' to 'stealing a veiw';[8] and Mrs. Robert Watson's impression of Emma's aunt as 'an old woman who gave all her money to an Irish Captain' becomes 'an old woman who threw herself away on an Irish Captain',[9] a revision which catches the meanness of her contempt. When Emma hears that Miss Edwards is engaged to dance with Captain Hunter she thinks 'poorly of her Brother's chances'; this is changed to make her consider 'her Brother Sam's a hopeless case',[10] the very idiom of her thought.

Many of the changes also serve to keep the narrative at its natural level, that is, in a neutral mode, between formality[11] and the familiar style of dialogue which occupies a large proportion of the fragment. Over a third of the novel is cast in direct speech, and some of the most interesting revisions are those

[1] p. 16, note to l. 20.
[2] p. 41, note to l. 7.
[3] p. 116, note to l. 5.
[4] p. 120, note to l. 15.
[5] In *Sense and Sensibility* Mrs. Dashwood is guilty of indifference to niceties of feeling and verbal usage when she proudly announces that she has 'never yet known what it was to separate esteem and love' (p. 16).
[6] p. 32, note to l. 12.
[7] p. 44, note to l. 21.
[8] p. 108, note to l. 5.
[9] p. 88, note to l. 10.
[10] p. 35, note to l. 19.
[11] e.g. pp. 117–19.

which introduce or mould an individual manner of expression. This process can be seen at work in the opening dialogue, where Elizabeth's muddle-headed, emotional good nature comes across to the reader in her description of the local society and the Watson family. Her manner of speech is modified by the slightest of alterations. Colloquial words and phrases replace a less familiar usage, e.g. 'I am rather afraid of' becomes 'I have my fears in that quarter';[1] 'I never met with anything so kind' becomes 'I never met with anything like it';[2] 'all the worse for poor Sam' becomes 'it is all over with poor Sam'.[3] A larger change points her tendency to turn to self-pity. She says of Penelope:

I wish she were well married with all my heart; when once she is, she will be a very worthy character—but till then . . .

This becomes:

I wish with all my heart she was well married. I declare I had rather have her well-married than myself.[4]

The reference to Penelope as 'a very worthy character' is removed, and the vehemence of Elizabeth's indignation against her sister is increased: 'She wd not deny it herself; she makes no secret of wishing to marry' becomes 'There is nothing she wd not do to get married—she would as good as tell you so herself.'[5]

The changes in Emma's speech are equally revealing. The basic qualities of her manner are good breeding and good sense, and Jane Austen is at pains to establish these traits in her telling rebuke to Lord Osborne.[6] In the corrected version she is endowed with courage, dignity and self-possession in admitting her straitened circumstances to a man whose interest in her seems patronizing and offensive. Accordingly, Lord Osborne's next approach—an invitation to the meet—is also changed, re-phrased in a more tentative form: 'I shall be hunting this Country next week' becomes 'My Hounds will be hunting';[7] 'I

---

[1] p. 16, note to l. 8.   [2] p. 15, note to l. 7.
[3] p. 16, note to l. 10.   [4] p. 7, note to l. 2.
[5] p. 6, note to l. 16.   [6] p. 79, note to l. 6.
[7] p. 82, note to l. 2.

hope you will be drawn out' becomes 'I mention this, in hopes of yr being drawn out';[1] 'If the morning's tolerable, do not be kept at home' becomes 'If the morning's tolerable, pray do us the honour of giving us your good wishes in person.'[2] And several lines of lively description, designed to attract Emma to the meet, are omitted: e.g. 'Everybody allows that there is not so fine a sight in the world as a pack of Fox-Hounds in full cry.'[3] Such warmth of expression is unsuited to Lord Osborne's awkwardness and formality of manner; it belongs rather to Tom Musgrave.

These revisions indicate Jane Austen's attempt to make the dialogue of the principals render contrasts of verbal expression, as well as differences, so defining the characters sharply in relationship to one another. On a smaller scale this design is seen in the alterations where Jane Austen distinguishes more finely among three kinds of egocentricity: the complacent self-satisfaction of Tom Musgrave,[4] the hypochondriac concerns of Mr. Watson[5] and the self-pity of Elizabeth.[6] As we see in the completed novels, unity of structure and effect is won partly through such a relationship of similarity or contrast among the characters; and, although this unity is not yet achieved in *The Watsons*, in the revision of dialogue we can observe Jane Austen working towards such an end.

The state of the manuscript confirms our impression that from the opening the plot and treatment were already decided and underwent no fundamental change during the writing or revision. Apart from the conversations of Emma and Lord Osborne[7] four other passages were heavily revised, yet the alteration is confined to matters of detail. The rather complicated action at the assembly is clarified, as are Emma's speech and movements with Charles immediately after their dance.[8] Jane Austen gives us a distinct impression of their individual

---

[1] p. 82, note to l. 5.
[2] p. 82, note to l. 8.
[3] p. 82, note to l. 7.
[4] p. 51, notes to ll. 20, 22.
[5] p. 73, note to l. 22; p. 74, note to l. 1.
[6] See above, p. 75.
[7] pp. 79–80, 81–82.
[8] pp. 44–48.

presences, while at the same time making them part of a larger
scene, a situation involving the movements, talk and thoughts of
other people. In the corrections to this passage we catch sight
of the work of construction that lies behind the assembly scenes
in *Northanger Abbey*, *Emma* and *Pride and Prejudice*, and other
episodes where such careful proportioning is required.

In the completed work the assembly would probably have
held as important a place as the ball scene in *Pride and Prejudice*
(where Elizabeth Bennet meets Darcy) and *Emma* (where the
heroine sees Mr. Knightley dance with Harriet Smith), for it
describes her first contact with the Osbornes, and may have
been the occasion on which Mr. Howard's admiration was to be
first aroused. Lord Osborne's and Tom Musgrave's visit to
Stanton is the second passage to be heavily revised.[1] Here
again the details of action and movement are clarified and
the reflections of Emma and Mr. Watson are made more
characteristic.[2] Tom Musgrave's second visit seems, however,
to have caused Jane Austen some difficulty. Perhaps she was
too intent on making his account of life at Osborne Castle
spirited and entertaining, for even after considerable revision
the passage[3] remains repetitive and confused. Finally, towards
the end of the fragment comes an account of Emma's situation
and her reflections on it[4] in a formal, almost grandiloquent
manner; this would probably have closed the first part of the
novel. The revision here shows Jane Austen raising the narrative
style with balanced sentences of pronounced rhythm, elevated
constructions, and diction in the tradition of Gibbon and
Johnson, a rhetoric very different from the simplicity of the
opening.

Miss Lascelles has observed that in *The Watsons* 'Jane Austen
seems to be struggling with a peculiar oppression, a stiffness
and heaviness that threaten her style'.[5] This comment is particularly appropriate to the closing section, where Emma's
thought is given an expansive and weighty form, far from the

[1] pp. 75–84. [2] pp. 83–84. [3] pp. 110–13.
[4] pp. 117–19. [5] *Jane Austen*, pp. 99–100.

distinctive wit and concentration of Jane Austen's practised manner. Miss Lascelles's observation might also be extended to other aspects of the work, namely, the portrayal of Emma and the progress of the action. One feels certain that Jane Austen was aware of these weaknesses. When she laid aside the fragment in 1805, it may well have been that the set-backs and grief of that time left her without the energy to struggle with such problems of style and technique.

5

THE *PLAN OF A NOVEL*

THE *Plan of a Novel, according to hints from various quarters*, written in 1816, is in the tradition of the childhood burlesques. There is no puzzle in Jane Austen's late return to the extravagance of her earliest writing. This kind of entertainment was revived for the benefit of the young nephews and nieces who so delighted to visit her at Chawton. One of those nieces, Caroline Austen, could recall occasions when her aunt would amuse the household, 'imagining for her neighbours impossible contingencies—by relating in prose or verse some trifling incident coloured to her own fancy, or in writing a history of what they had said or done, that *could* deceive nobody'.[1] With Caroline's elder sister, Anna, Jane Austen used to enjoy ridiculing the latest novels from the circulating library at Alton,[2] and in 1814 this joking developed into a mock correspondence.[3] In November or December of that year Jane Austen told Anna that she hoped to write 'a close Imitation'[4] of Mary Brunton's *Self Control* (1811), a novel which she had glanced at three years before, finding it 'an excellently-meant, elegantly-written Work, without anything of Nature or Probability in it. I declare I do not know whether Laura's passage down the American River is not the most natural, possible, everyday thing she ever does.'[5] There is no evidence that the promised imitation was ever written; the idea of such a burlesque was probably just a passing fancy which remained dormant until the writing of the *Plan*, where once again we encounter the allusive humour of

[1] *My Aunt*, p. 8.
[2] Anna recorded these details, of the period c. 1812–13, which are quoted from family manuscripts by Hill, p. 195.
[3] *Letters*, p. 406.   [4] Ibid., p. 423.
[5] Ibid., p. 344.

the juvenilia, the oblique references to the family life and reading, together with a comic exposé of the improbabilities of
romantic fiction. Yet now it is the critical voice of a practised
novelist, and in the *Plan* and the correspondence from which it
arose, we have the most important account of what Jane Austen
understood to be her aims and capacities as a novelist.

The occasion for this joke was her meeting with the Rev.
James Stanier Clarke, Librarian to the Prince Regent. The
autumn of 1815 she spent in London with Henry Austen at
Hans Place. During her stay he fell dangerously ill and was
attended by one of the court physicians. Learning of Jane
Austen's presence in the house[1] the doctor passed the news
back to the Regent; and he later informed her 'that the Prince
was a great admirer of her novels: that he often read them,
and had a set in each of his residences'.[2] The day after this
flattering report she was waited on by Clarke, carrying an invitation for her to see over Carlton House, which she duly visited
on 13 November. During the visit Clarke intimated that she was
at liberty to dedicate her next work to his royal master. As *Emma*
was then in the press she wrote immediately for confirmation
of this honour. Clarke at once reassured her on the point. He
continued his letter with the suggestion that she might care 'to
delineate in some future Work the Habits of Life and Character
and enthusiasm of a Clergyman . . . Fond of, & entirely engaged in Literature',[3] an idealized portrait, in fact, of the librarian
himself. Jane Austen replied firmly and modestly that she was
incapable of drawing such a figure: 'The comic part of the
character I might be equal to, but not the good, the enthusiastic,
the literary.'[4] She insisted that she lacked the education to make
his conversation sufficiently learned. Clarke was not put off by
this polite evasion. Set upon literary immortality, he tried again

---

[1] The authorship of the three novels so far published was unacknowledged
on the title-pages, although, according to Caroline Austen, 'her name had
been made public enough' (*My Aunt*, p. 12). Henry had broken this secret
more than once before, 'in the warmth of his Brotherly vanity & Love', as Jane
Austen termed his indiscretion (*Letters*, p. 340, to Francis, 25 September 1813).

[2] *My Aunt*, p. 12.   [3] *Letters*, p. 430 (no. 113*a*, 16 November 1815).

[4] Ibid., p. 443 (no. 120, 11 December).

to 'elicit' her 'Genius',[1] offering more aspects of his own career
—his experience as a naval chaplain, and at court—to be in
cluded in this portrait of an English clergyman. Indignation
as well as vanity prompted the librarian: 'describe him burying
his own mother—as I did—because the High Priest of the
Parish in which she died—did not pay her remains the respect
he ought to do. I have never recovered from the Shock.'[2]

Perhaps this letter embarrassed Jane Austen; there is no
record of an answer, and we hear next of the matter three
months later. For the third time he asked her to attempt a
story close to his own affairs.[3] He advised that 'any historical
romance, illustrative of the history of the august House of
Cobourg' (to which he had been recently appointed) 'would just
now be very interesting',[4] the marriage of Prince Leopold and
Princess Charlotte being near at hand. In the *Plan* there is no
mention of historical romance, which might well have been
introduced as a point of additional ridiculousness, not at all
incongruous in the story of a 'present day'[5] clergyman which
anyway concludes on a farcical and contradictory note. Probably
by this time, the end of March 1816, the *Plan* was already
written. Jane Austen thanked the librarian for his advice and
again excused herself, pleading that she 'could no more write
a romance than an epic poem. . . . No, I must keep to my own
style and go on in my own way; and though I may never succeed
again in that, I am convinced that I should totally fail in any
other.'[6] Even if Clarke got no satisfaction, his badgering had
provoked Jane Austen to a serious estimate of the capabilities
and limitations which fitted her to draw, as she modestly put it,
'pictures of domestic life in country villages' from which she
would not be tempted by 'profit or popularity'.[7]

However, as we know, the correspondence did bear fruit.
The account of her meeting with the librarian was already a joke
at Hans Place. Caroline records that 'My Aunt, soon after her

---

[1] Ibid., p. 445 (no. 120*a* (? 21) December).   [2] Ibid., pp. 444–5.
[3] Ibid., no. 126*a* (27 March 1816).   [4] Ibid., p. 451.
[5] p. 430.   [6] pp. 452–3 (Letter 126, 1 April).   [7] p. 452.

visit to *him*, returned home, where the little adventure was talked of for a while with some interest, and afforded some amusement'.[1] Unknown to Clarke she adopted his original proposal as the nucleus of her comic *Plan*, taking over suggestions almost verbatim from his two letters, and in appearance at least, also following the idea that she should urge her friends to provide material. In the margin she identifies the 'various quarters' from which the 'hints' came. This, of course, is in elaboration of the joke, Jane Austen's way of having some private fun at the expense of her critics. Apart from Mrs. Pearse (of whom nothing is known), the other six contributors had already taken an interest in her writing. William Gifford read *Emma* for Murray and offered to revise the book in proof.[2] If his offer was passed on to the author, probably she refused it as politely and firmly as she rejected Clarke's suggestions. All the other contributors had made some comment on *Emma* or *Mansfield Park*.[3] Mr. Sherer, Vicar of Godmersham (whom she met on visits to her brother Edward), echoes Clarke with a proposal that the clergyman be 'the model of an exemplary Parish Priest'.[4] Jane Austen was getting her own back on Sherer for his recent censure of *Emma*: 'did not think it equal to either *MP*—(which he liked the best of all) or *P&P.*—Displeased with my pictures of Clergymen.'[5] Other suggestions may have been solicited: Fanny Knight was her favourite niece; Henry Sanford was an acquaintance of Henry Austen; Mary Cooke a second cousin; and Mrs. Craven a close family friend. Some of these probably offered suggestions in full knowledge that they were contributing to an elaborate joke.

Joining their 'hints' to those of Clarke (from Letters 113*a* and 120*a*), Jane Austen formed the *Plan*, which strikes at the extravagance, melodrama and unreality of romantic stories. Jane Austen now proposes, by way of mocking imitation, to draw

---

[1] *My Aunt*, pp. 12–13.
[2] Letter to John Murray, 29 September 1815 (Samuel Smiles, *A Publisher and His Friends* (1891), i. 282).
[3] *Opinions of Emma, Opinions of Mansfield Park*, printed with *Plan of a Novel*, pp. 13–23.   [4] p. 10.   [5] p. 20.

'pictures of perfection':[1] the clergyman an exemplary curate, the heroine of 'faultless Character',[2] with every accomplishment, the Grandisonian hero 'all perfection of course—& only prevented from paying his addresses to her, by some excess of refinement'.[3] The wicked 'will be completely depraved & infamous'.[4] The dialogue of the father and daughter is to be in 'long speeches, elegant Language',[5] while the *Plan* itself is cast in a curious hybrid style, much of its diction and phraseology 'thorough novel slang',[6] mingled with colloquialisms, in sentences that vary from elliptical notes to elaborate and balanced periods.

A familiar device, the life-story, is to occupy much of the first volume, which closes with the clergyman's 'opinion of the Benefits to result from Tythes being done away',[7] one of Clarke's suggestions,[8] the sort 'of solemn specious nonsense, about something unconnected with the story'[9] that Jane Austen had once offered to Cassandra as an improvement to *Pride and Prejudice*. She was here referring to the contemporary practice of using fiction as a vehicle for political and philosophical propaganda, for the doctrines of Rousseau and revolutionary liberalism, or as a means of moral and educational improvement. This was something to be endured or laughed at in the novels of Maria Edgeworth,[10] or in Scott, whose 'History of the Hartz Demon'

[1] *Letters*, pp. 486–7: 'pictures of perfection as you know make me sick & wicked'; to Fanny Knight, 23 March 1817. Perhaps this is an allusion to the *Plan*, with which her niece was probably familiar.
[2] p. 9. This 'hint' is credited to Fanny Knight.
[3] pp. 10–11. [4] p. 10. [5] p. 9.
[6] Writing to Anna Austen about a character in the girl's novel she advises: '. . . I wish you would not let him plunge into a "vortex of Dissipation". I do not object to the Thing, but I cannot bear the expression;—it is such thorough novel slang—and so old, that I dare say Adam met with it in the first novel he opened' (*Letters*, p. 404). [7] p. 10.
[8] *Letters*, p. 444. [9] Ibid., pp. 299–300.
[10] The freedom of Jane Austen's work from such discursive and inartistic material was remarked upon at the time. In August 1814 the first Earl of Dudley (John William Ward) wrote to a friend that he had just begun *Mansfield Park*. He continued: 'I am a great admirer of the two other works by the same author. She has not so much fine humour as your friend Miss Edgeworth, but she is more skilful in contriving a story, she has a great deal more feeling, and she never plagues you with any chemistry, mechanics, or political economy, which are all excellent things in their way, but vile,

she found so amusing in *The Antiquary*.[1] True to the scope of
romance the story is to contain 'a striking variety of adventures
. . . a wide variety of Characters',[2] as the father and daughter
move about Europe pursued by the anti-hero, until at the closing
stages the humour rises to a note of hilarious nonsense. The
father 'after 4 or 5 hours of tender advice & parental Admoni-
tion . . . expires in a fine burst of Literary Enthusiasm'.[3]
Although the daughter is 'now & then starved to death'[4] and
driven to Kamschatka, Jane Austen adds, in flat contradiction,
'Throughout the whole work, Heroine to be in the most elegant
Society & living in high style.'[5] This last stipulation was perhaps
in answer to a note entreating her to add another volume to
Mansfield Park; the anonymous correspondent 'laments that
his acquaintance with persons so amiable and elegant in mind
and manners is of so short duration'.[6] Dr. Chapman dates this
scrap *c.* 1815 and suggests that it could have been written by her
nephew, James Edward Austen. Another family joke may be in
the description of the heroine's 'dark eyes & plump cheeks'.[7]
In the letters[8] there are many approving references to dark eyes,
and all the family portraits[9] reveal these as characteristic of the
Austens, although Jane Austen's eyes are described as hazel.[10]

Like the juvenilia this piece is both entertainment and
criticism, none the less acute for being delivered in fun. The
juvenilia burlesques foreshadowed Jane Austen's development,
largely by showing what she was not going to write, whereas
the *Plan* has the experience of four completed novels behind it,
and details otherwise unremarkable gain a new significance in
the light of her earlier writing. For instance, the predicament

cold-hearted trash in a novel. . . .' (Letter of 11 August 1814, *Letters to Ivy
from the First Earl of Dudley* (1905), ed. S. H. Romilly, p. 250).
    ¹ Letter to James Edward Austen, 16 December 1816 (*Letters*, p. 468).
    ² p. 10.   ³ p. 11.   ⁴ Ibid.   ⁵ Ibid.   ⁶ *Critical Bibliography*, pp. 20–21.
    ⁷ p. 9.   ⁸ e.g. pp. 87, 91, 193, 236–7, 286, 345, 479.
    ⁹ See the portraits reproduced in Hill; and in J. H. and E. Hubback,
Jane Austen's Sailor Brothers (1906) (see especially the pencil drawing of her
sister by Cassandra, reproduced opposite p. 226, and discussed by Dr. Chapman in *Facts and Problems*, pp. 212–13).
    ¹⁰ 1870 *Memoir*, p. 106; see also Caroline Austen's description in *My Aunt*,
p. 5.

of the Dashwoods, the Bennets, the Watsons, the Bertrams, and the Prices is largely due to the shortcomings or absence of the head of the family, a situation which exposes the characters to pressures of circumstance and moral strains, without any recourse to violence of action. By contrast, the clergyman in the *Plan* is 'without the smallest drawback or peculiarity to prevent his being the most delightful companion to his Daughter from one year's end to the other'.[1] Given such a father and a perfect heroine the action and interest must arise from remarkable external events, not from the revelation and shaping of character. The 'Good' are to be entirely free from those 'foibles or weaknesses'[2] which individualize people in life and art. On the other hand, a more discriminating characterization is signified by her use of the term 'Anti-hero',[3] rather than villain, for a young man 'totally unprincipled & heart-less',[4] a version of the opportunists Willoughby, John Thorpe, Wickham and Crawford, whose failings, to a lesser degree, are essentially of this kind. The anti-hero's female counterpart is the young woman 'of Talents & Shrewdness'[4] from whose acquaintance the heroine shrinks, as the heroines of the novels turn from Lucy Steele, Isabella Thorpe, the Bingley sisters, Mary Crawford and Mrs. Elton.

Jane Austen's first aim in the *Plan* was to make fun of Clarke and to use his suggestions in a family entertainment, drawing friends and relations into the joke. In doing so she also expressed her amused contempt for popular fiction, with its rigid black and white characters, its melodramatic action, episodic plots, and lack of structural coherence. Read in conjunction with the letters of advice to Anna,[5] who was also engaged in writing, the *Plan* and its accompanying correspondence stress the principles which Jane Austen maintained so consistently in the six novels, presenting the subject-matter of observed and familiar life with naturalness and probability, an essential fidelity to common experience, without which her higher aims could never have been achieved.

[1] p. 9.   [2] p. 10.   [3] p. 11.   [4] p. 10.
[5] Letters 95, 98, 100, 101, 107, May or June to December 1814.

6

THE TWO CHAPTERS OF *PERSUASION*

THE two chapters of *Persuasion* is the only fragment to have survived from the writing of the novels. It is a thirty-two page draft of what, at one stage, was to have been the ending of the work, chapters 10 and 11 in the second volume. The manuscript, corrected and revised, is dated at several places, and with the help of the final, printed text, we are able to observe in every detail the changes that Jane Austen made to the close of the story, sections of which can be examined in three states: in the wording of the original; above that the corrected and revised version; this, in turn, can be compared with the text of 1818, which contains further alterations.[1] The manuscript provides evidence of her attention to the minutiae of verbal effects (as in *The Watsons* and *Sanditon*); it also reveals how the treatment of the story's ending underwent a complete change. Even as an experienced and successful writer Jane Austen's conception and execution were neither instinctive nor unerring. We feel the inevitable rightness in her handling of the novel's conclusion; yet this achievement was not, in the act of creation, a swift and effortless performance, but a triumph of rethinking won through trial and error. In comparing this manuscript with the completed work we come as close as possible to following the process of her imagination. Henry James found her novels 'instinctive and charming' and declared that 'For signal examples of what composition, distribution, arrangement can do, of how they intensify the life of a work of art, we have to go elsewhere'.[2]

[1] *Persuasion* was published after Jane Austen's death. Whether she would have made further revisions to the story is an open question; it is almost certain that some changes were made by the publishers or printers (see below, pp. 97n., 98n.), as well as by Henry in proof-reading. We can assume that the text does not represent her intention in every detail.

[2] 'Gustave Flaubert' (1902), in *The House of Fiction* (1957), ed. Leon Edel, p. 207.

Apparently James knew nothing of the two chapters. Whatever may be true of the finished novels is not true of this manuscript, from which we receive a very different impression; indeed, it provides a signal example of that conscious art which James was always seeking.

The place of this manuscript in the composition of *Persuasion* can be established almost exactly. The novel was written between 8 August 1815 and 6 August 1816;[1] and the first sheet of the manuscript chapter 10 is dated 8 July 1816. Eight days later chapter 11 was finished, and at that time Jane Austen considered the work satisfactorily completed, as we see by the date and the word 'Finis' written at the foot of 14^r. Almost immediately she had second thoughts. 'Finis' and 'July 16 1816' were erased for the addition of a further paragraph on 14^v,[2] after which is written 'Finis July 18. 1816'. Of the single gathering of sixteen leaves the last two still remained unused. Then, on these blank leaves, Jane Austen wrote another five hundred words to be inserted in chapter 10, marking an X in the margin where they were to be added. This extra material, undated, is in a hand similar to that of the body of the manuscript and was probably written very soon afterwards.

The manuscript was first mentioned and its contents described (misleadingly) in the 1870 *Memoir*.[3] By this account Jane Austen is said to have 'cancelled the condemned chapter', and to have written two others, 'entirely different, in its stead'.[4] This description fails to make it clear that more than a quarter of the original chapter 10 was incorporated almost verbatim in the new chapter 11,[5] and that the manuscript consists of a further chapter (the original chapter 11) which was taken over in the completed work (as chapter 12) with some changes to the wording. In the 1871 *Memoir* chapter 10 alone was printed,[6]

---

[1] Dated by Jane Austen; see her note, reproduced in *Plan of a Novel*, p. 36.　　　　　　　　　　[2] *Two Chapters*, p. 38, note to l. 17.
[3] pp. 218–20.　　　　　　　　　　　　　　　　　　　　　[4] p. 219.
[5] *Two Chapters*, p. 18, l. 7 to p. 25, l. 16 corresponds to *Persuasion*, pp. 241–5.
[6] pp. 167–80, 'now printed, in compliance with the requests addressed to me from several quarters' (J. E. Austen-Leigh's note, p. 158).

still with no indication that this was only a part of the manuscript. Both chapters were presented fully and accurately, for the first time, in Dr. Chapman's edition of 1926.

The rewriting of chapter 10 provides the most important evidence in the history of correction and revision behind the finished work. It points directly to the special problems of treatment and construction that faced Jane Austen at the end of *Persuasion*. In turning this section into the present chapter 11 she entirely changed the reunion, transforming the setting and action, investing it with the tone and mood which prevail throughout the novel, qualities which had escaped her in writing the first version.

The original chapter 10 is a comedy scene, wholly out of keeping with the seriousness and emotional intensity required of the novel's climax. The circumstances of the reunion are clumsily devised, in the manner of a stage farce. The Admiral and Mrs. Croft, hitherto an ideal couple, paragons of warmhearted and unpretentious good sense, are forced out of character. They behave like a pair of sly matchmakers, although at heart they are unchanged. Anne and Wentworth, too, are presented in a new and wholly uncharacteristic light. For much of the chapter they are caught up by circumstances, seemingly deprived of that very power of rational and independent action that is vital to the definition of their characters and to the meaning of the work. They are thrown off balance by a series of surprises and misunderstandings, contrived incidents which fail to arise naturally out of character or the existing order of events. Anne is tempted into the house on the assurance that there is no one inside except Mrs. Croft and the mantua-maker; no deception on the Admiral's part, as he regards Wentworth, his brother-in-law, as one of the family. Wentworth blunders by pure chance onto the discovery that Anne still loves him. This fact emerges accidentally when, at the Admiral's direction, he is inquiring whether the Kellynch lease is to be cancelled on her marriage to Walter Elliot. This mistake is only one of a number of disconcerting events which sweep away Anne's reserve, and finally bring to light their continuing affection, an exposure rather than a revelation of feeling, a process of discovery which may be true to life but not to the life of *Persuasion*, whose probability is violated in this chapter.[1] In this treatment the major statement of the book is confused: Anne's fitness to judge and over-ride Lady Russell's objections to her marriage, the 'persuasion' which formerly kept her from Wentworth.

This failure begins at the opening of the chapter, in the portrayal of Anne's mental confusion. She has just learnt the truth about Walter Elliot from Mrs. Smith:

> The Embarrassment which must be felt from this hour in his presence!—How to behave to him?—how to get rid of him?—what to do by any of Party at home?—where to be blind? where to be active? It was altogether a confusion of Images & Doubts—a perplexity, an agitation which she could not see the end of.[2]

The new perplexity of thought and feeling is well conveyed; however, like the action which follows, it is totally unsuited to the evolution of character and meaning already set in progress by the rest of the book.[3] Yet the light correction and revision of chapter 10 indicate that at the time of writing Jane Austen was quite satisfied with the scene in the Admiral's house. The alterations, like those in *The Watsons*, strengthen elements already present in the original draft, sustaining the vigour of a chapter already alive with action, movement and spirited dialogue. The force of the style is maintained by economy and precision in the diction, and in these changes we can see Jane Austen's working for expressiveness and emphatic definition: 'said' becomes 'denied',[4] 'saying' becomes 'calling out',[5] 'with

---

[1] In reviewing *Northanger Abbey* and *Persuasion* Whateley observed that the novels 'have all that compactness of plan and unity of action which is generally produced by a sacrifice of probability: yet they have little or nothing that is not probable' (*Quarterly Review*, xxiv (1821), 224).   [2] pp. 3–4.

[3] L. D. Cohen ('Insight, the Essence of Jane Austen's Artistry', *Nineteenth-Century Fiction*, iv (1954), 272–89) examining changes made to the end of *Persuasion* fails to make the point that for its immediate purpose the style of the manuscript chapter 10 is perfectly adequate; one (though not the only) reason that the present chapter 11 seems better written is its fitness to the work as a whole.

[4] p. 4, note to l. 11.   [5] p. 4, note to l. 15.

determined spirit' becomes 'with a more passive Determination',[1] 'hear' becomes 'distinguish'.[2] The few changes in the dialogue maintain the colloquial manner. For example, the Admiral's remark to Anne, 'But I do not see much the look of it in your Countenance' becomes 'But you have not much the Look of it—as Grave as a little Judge'.[3] The only important revision is an adjustment to Anne's character. Having heard the truth about Walter Elliot from Mrs. Smith, she is

pained for Lady Russell & glancing with composed Complacency & Lenient (?) Triumph upon the fact of her having been right & Lady R. wrong herself the most discriminating of the two. *She* had never been satisfied. Lady Russell's confidence had been entire.

Such a feeling of complacent triumph is wholly inconsistent with the justice and generosity of Anne's nature, and Jane Austen removed the sting of these reflections, leaving the manuscript to read 'and pained for Lady Russell, whose confidence in him had been entire'.[4]

The first sign that Jane Austen was at all uneasy about this account is the addition, at the end of the manuscript, after the completion of chapter 11, of a passage for insertion in chapter 10.[5] Perhaps she felt that the treatment of Anne and Wentworth had been a trifle perfunctory, and that their character analysis should be more obviously linked to the theme announced in the work's title. Within this section Wentworth is now made to recall to Anne the pain and despair he experienced on seeing her in the company of William Walter Elliot and Lady Russell at the concert. This sight, he tells her, suggested to him that 'persuasion' might work against him once again, as it had done eight years before. In Anne's reply Jane Austen draws together the dominant themes of 'persuasion' and 'duty', giving these very words to the heroine as she explains her conduct.

This additional section is included in the portion of chapter 10 that Jane Austen transposed to the setting of the new chapter 11,

[1] p. 8, note to l. 17.   [2] p. 9, note to l. 16.
[3] p. 6, notes to ll. 2, 3.   [4] p. 3, note to l. 8.
[5] Between p. 22, l. 12, and p. 25, l. 19.

where the reunion takes place in the White Hart. Wentworth
blames himself with increased frankness and force for his previous obstinacy and pride. The change of reported into direct
speech[1] heightens the vehemence of self-condemnation as he
acknowledges the thoughtlessness of his behaviour with Louisa
Musgrove. The concluding sentence, newly added, makes the
point unequivocally: 'I had been grossly wrong, and must abide
the consequences.'[2] Another slight alteration illustrates the way
in which Jane Austen deepens the characterization of Anne and
Wentworth, and relates their present experiences to those of
the past. The manuscript reads,

Before they parted at night, Anne had the felicity of being assured
in the first place that—(so far from being altered for the worse!)—
she had *gained* inexpressibly in personal Loveliness . . .[3]

In the corresponding section of the 1818 text Wentworth tells
her that during his stay with Edward, his brother

'enquired after you very particularly; asked even if you were personally altered, little suspecting that to my eye you could never alter.'
    Anne smiled, and let it pass. It was too pleasing a blunder for
a reproach. It is something for a woman to be assured, in her eight-
and-twentieth year, that she has not lost one charm of earlier youth:
but the value of such homage was inexpressibly increased to Anne,
by comparing it with former words, and feeling it to be the result,
not the cause of a revival of his warm attachment.[4]

The innocent flattery of a lover's adoration, received by Anne
(at first) with a touch of ironic surprise, becomes, in the final
version, an example of Jane Austen's artistic fidelity to life.
Wentworth's 'blunder', the thoughtless slip of the tongue which
can plague us at any time, affects even the hero at his happiest
moment, and evokes the generosity of Anne's love.
    But not until we compare the two chapters in their entirety
do we see the full contrast between an unremarkable (but not

[1] *Two Chapters*, p. 20, l. 6 to p. 21, l. 5 becomes *Persuasion*, pp. 242–3.
[2] *Persuasion*, p. 243.
[3] *Two Chapters*, p. 18.   [4] *Persuasion*, p. 243.

unrepresentative) piece of writing and a passage of extraordinary beauty, unequalled in her other works. According to the 1870 *Memoir* she was keenly aware of the weaknesses in her first version: 'She thought it tame and flat, and was desirous of producing something better.'[1] This problem seems to have weighed upon her until one morning, some days later, 'she awoke to more cheerful views and brighter inspiration: the sense of power revived; and imagination resumed its course'.[2] It might be a matter for surprise that an artist so experienced, who could write the entire novel in twelve months, and at a time when her health was failing, should fall so far short in her first design. Some of its flaws have already been discussed, while the tameness and flatness which the *Memoir* refers to can be identified with the central episode, the conversation between the Admiral and Wentworth, and the dialogue between Wentworth and Anne. This has a second-hand air; the noisily conducted conversation, unwittingly overheard by an interested third party, is a well-worn device in drama and fiction, and Anne has already played the role of hidden listener behind the hedge at Winthrop, as Wentworth lectured Louisa Musgrove. The conversation at cross-purposes, an equally familiar comic situation (belittled in *Emma*, mocked at in *Northanger Abbey*, and neatly cut short in *Sense and Sensibility*), is the cause of Anne's uncertainty about the point of Wentworth's inquiry.

As the *Memoir* suggests fatigue and ill health may have interfered with Jane Austen's performance. Yet this cannot explain her difficulty in matching the scene of reunion with the rest of the work. I believe that the problem was really a technical matter. For the first time she was constructing a dramatic and emotional climax, an intensification of the heroine's experience, achieved suddenly, and in circumstances that affect her whole future. The arrival of Willoughby at Cleveland, and his confession to Elinor is a moment of high drama; Catherine's

[1] p. 218.
[2] pp. 218–19. According to the dates we have (see above, p. 87), the rewriting of the two chapters could not have taken more than nineteen days.

adventures at Northanger and her dismissal by General Tilney are sudden and exciting events. However, these episodes, like the accident to Louisa Musgrove, are incidental to the story; they are not the resolution of the entire work, as the reunion of Anne and Wentworth is. In *Persuasion* Jane Austen is using this structural pattern, a combination of climax and resolution, for the first time, and in this respect chapter 10 can be regarded as a trial, rather than a failure.

At first the climax was created from surprise and mis-understanding, excitements deriving largely from events within the chapter. Then she probably recognized that the reunion was cut off from the rest of the work by this discordant element of broad comedy. In rewriting the scene she adjusts it to the tone, the sequence of events, and the rhythm of action already established in the story. The pressure of interest and feeling here is the product and culmination of the entire work; not merely a local element, but the consequence of all that we have seen Anne to suffer and endure. At this stage the reader is pain-fully concerned for Anne's happiness, for her uncertainty to be eased, and Jane Austen saw that there was no need to force the pace of the action, or to introduce the drama of events into a situation already so charged with feeling. She shapes a climax which concentrates on the relationship of Anne and Wentworth, and avoids the irrelevant interests that weakened the first ver-sion. The scene, action, and dialogue are designed to prove that the couple are now 'more tender, more tried, more fixed in a knowledge of each other's character, truth, and attachment; more equal to act, more justified in acting'.[1] The course of Anne's experience has shown her that while she could have married eight years ago, in defiance of Lady Russell's 'per-suasion', she was right to accept guidance and acknowledge the higher obligations of 'duty'. The new chapter 11 resolves the moral drama, revealing that Anne and Wentworth are now wholly justified in marriage. In the manuscript chapter, how-ever, the intensity and reasonableness of their love are not

[1] *Persuasion*, pp. 240–1.

communicated, nor do they come together with a full understanding of the past, whereas chapter 11 exhibits their powers
of self-determination, their consciousness in every thought,
feeling, and act.

At the White Hart there is an air of outward calm and
spaciousness, in contrast to the confusion and excitement of
the events which threw them together in the Admiral's house.
The five people are carefully arranged about the room. The
scene is highly pictured. Through the observation of movement,
speech, and reaction, we are kept aware of the separate identities.
The device of the overheard conversation is used again; formerly
Anne overheard Wentworth, now Wentworth overhears Anne,
and instead of confusion and misunderstanding there is clarity
and insight. The discussion between Mrs. Musgrove and Mrs.
Croft on early marriage and Anne's plea for the constancy of
woman's love touch Wentworth deeply; the first is the one
objection that formerly stood in their way, the second is the
one remaining doubt that has troubled him until this moment.
Thus his proposal (which Jane Austen gives freely and fully
in a letter) arises naturally and rationally out of the progress of
the action. From this point Anne's waiting is over, a little later
Wentworth too is calmed, and Jane Austen relaxes the emotional
intensity. Lightening their serious review of the past is a controlled lyrical note, the glow of romantic love that Anne 'learned
. . . as she grew older'.[1]

The chapter closes with Wentworth's admission that having
once been refused by Anne, 'I shut my eyes, and would not
understand you, or do you justice.'[2] His honest self-scrutiny
reassures us that he will be a fit husband, and he ends on a
note of unsuspected wit: 'Like other great men under reverses
. . . I must endeavour to subdue my mind to my fortune. I must
learn to brook being happier than I deserve.'[3] Tactfully, Jane
Austen withdraws our attention from Anne Elliot; her story is
told. At the close of chapter 10 there is no such delicacy. Anne
found that

[1] *Persuasion*, p. 30.   [2] p. 247.   [3] Ibid.

It was necessary to sit up half the Night, & lie awake the remainder to comprehend with composure her present state, & pay for the overplus of Bliss, by Headake and Fatigue.[1]

Anne was treated lightly, like a Catherine Morland, or a Marianne Dashwood, not as she truly is, a mature woman—if not the favourite among Jane Austen's heroines, surely the noblest, as we see in the new chapter 11, where the passage is completely changed:

An interval of meditation, serious and grateful, was the best corrective of every thing dangerous in such high-wrought felicity; and she went to her room, and grew steadfast and fearless in the thankfulness of her enjoyment.[2]

When 'the sense of power revived; and imagination resumed its course',[3] Jane Austen replaced the manuscript version, flawed in detail as it is in general design, with a chapter that matches the delicate power of the theme, action, and characters. As Conrad saw it, the art of fiction is to seize 'a passing phase of life . . . to show its vibration, its colour, its form; and through its movement, its form, and its colour, reveal the substance of its truth—disclose its inspiring secret: the stress and passion within the core of each convincing moment.'[4] Nowhere else in her writing does Jane Austen seize upon a more profound 'phase of life'; and nowhere else is the 'stress and passion . . . of each convincing moment' disclosed so surely.

With little change the draft chapter 11 becomes chapte 12 in the printed text. The slight alterations on the manuscript sustain the economy, precision, and vitality of the style. For example, the rather heavy phrase 'bear down all opposition' becomes 'carry their point',[5] 'it was pretty evident on what terms they had previously been' becomes 'it was evident how double a Game he had been playing',[6] 'overspread her Sunshine' becomes 'dim her Sunshine'.[7] Some of the major alterations are

[1] *Two Chapters*, p. 27.   [2] *Persuasion*, p. 245.
[3] 1870 *Memoir*, p. 219.
[4] Preface to *The Nigger of the Narcissus* (1897), Dent, 1950, p. x.
[5] p. 29, note to l. 5.
[6] p. 35, note to l. 11.   [7] p. 39, note to l. 14.

in the adjustment of tone, as if in anticipation of the graver mood which was to control the design of the new chapter 11, yet to be written. It is Jane Austen's custom to conclude her stories ironically, with a hasty and deliberately undramatic settlement of events, as she does here. But as if already conscious of the need to treat her story more seriously than in the previous chapter, she modifies her pose of indifference to the remaining threads of the plot. The ironic tone at the opening of the chapter is lightened as soon as written: 'Who can want to hear anything further?' is changed immediately to 'Who can be in doubt of what followed?'[1] And later, the irony that she originally allowed to play upon the theme of *Persuasion* is removed altogether. Before alteration the manuscript reads:

> Bad Morality again. A young Woman proved to have had more discrimination of Character than her elder—to have seen in two Instances more clearly what it was about than her God-mother! But on the point of Morality, I confess myself almost in despair after understanding myself to have already given a Mother offence— having already appeared weak in the point where I thought myself most strong and shall leave the present matter to the mercy of Mothers & Chaperons & Middle-aged Ladies in general . . .[2]

The reference in the third sentence, to already having 'given a Mother offence', sounds as if a family joke has been allowed to creep in, as if this is a reminder of a discussion of *Persuasion* or other of her works among the household or friends;[3] and we know from their *Opinions* of *Emma* and *Mansfield Park*[4] that criticism was readily offered. But Jane Austen cancelled this passage in favour of another,[5] completely free from irony and private allusion, to make the distinction (vital to the theme) between 'natural Penetration' and 'Experience'[6] in the judgement of character.

The other major changes strengthen the relationship of this

---

[1] p. 29, note to l. 1.   [2] p. 32, note to l. 17.
[3] Her niece Marianne Knight recalls that Jane Austen always brought her current manuscript on visits to the Knight family home at Godmersham and would read to the elder daughters (quoted by Hill, p. 202).
[4] *Plan of a Novel*, pp. 13–23.   [5] pp. 32–33.   [6] p. 32.

chapter to earlier parts of the book. The passage describing Sir Walter Elliot's opinion of Wentworth and the marriage is heavily worked over.[1] The sentence form is greatly improved and a significant detail is introduced: Sir Walter was able 'at last to prepare his pen with a very good grace for the insertion of the Marriage in the volume of Honour'.[2] This is an extension of the joke we have on the first page of the book, an echo that contributes, however slightly, to its unity of structure.

The ending also caused Jane Austen some difficulty. First, she cancelled her original last four lines; and then, in turn, cancelled the substituted passage[3] in favour of a new concluding paragraph[4] added two days later. This extends the reference to Mrs. Smith and links her more closely to the fortunes of Anne and Wentworth. There is evidence to suggest that *Persuasion* may not have been finally revised, and I believe that these second thoughts at the end of the manuscript betray Jane Austen's uneasiness about Mrs. Smith's place in the story.

There are fifteen points (apart from the removal of italics and capitals[5]) at which the 1818 text differs from the revised manuscript. These changes, like many of those to the manuscript of the original chapter, are slight adjustments to style which show, if nothing else, the degree of attention that Jane Austen paid to the smallest detail of syntax, sentence structure, and diction. For example, 'assisted by (*for* together with) his well-sounding name',[6] 'The only one (*for* person) among them',[7] 'she might flatter herself with having (*for* that she had) been greatly instrumental to the connexion, by keeping Anne (*for* having Anne staying) with her in the autumn',[8] 'fully requited the services *which* (*added*) she had rendered'.[9] These changes

---

[1] p. 30, note to l. 22 becomes *Persuasion*, pp. 248–9. [2] p. 31.
[3] p. 38, note to l. 17. [4] pp. 38–39.
[5] Dr. Chapman suggests that the italics of the manuscript 'in the print of 1818 may have been suppressed beyond the author's intention' (*Two Chapters*, Preface). This may also be true of the capitalization, which is significant for the emphasis it places upon terms such as Persuasion, Duty, Experience. [6] *Persuasion*, p. 248, cf. *Two Chapters*, p. 31.
[7] *Persuasion*, p. 249, cf. *Two Chapters*, p. 31.
[8] *Persuasion*, p. 249, cf. *Two Chapters*, p. 33.
[9] *Persuasion*, p. 252, cf. *Two Chapters*, p. 38.

are typical of Jane Austen's manner of revision, and I think that
we may assume that she was responsible (rather than Henry
Austen, the publisher's reader,[1] or the proof-reader) for variations, apart from those of typographical style, between the
manuscript and the printed text.

The cancelled chapters are our only direct evidence for Jane
Austen's method of composition in the completed novels. In
chapter 10 her structural technique is at an important moment of
development as she experiments, at first to fail, with the crucial
scene, a climax and resolution, which must raise the dramatic
and emotional intensity, and then lead on to the moments of
relief and peace. Making her mistakes in the first version Jane
Austen went on to recast the chapter, visualizing the scene with
great clarity. To place people within the enclosed setting of a
room, at rest or in movement, to record their conversation, and
to concentrate above all on a delicate sense of relationship, their
awareness of one another, spoken and unspoken, these are the
feats of her art, here and in the other works.

As a climax chapter 11 is something new in the structure of
the novels, but its set-piece effects are gained with techniques
practised throughout her career. It is therefore not surprising to
find that the manuscript chapter 11 (without any such problems)
fits into the design of the finished work, as chapter 12, with little
change. From this, and our knowledge that *Persuasion* was
written in almost exactly twelve months, we can conclude that
as a practised writer Jane Austen was able to realize her intentions at an early stage in the composition of her work. We may
regret the loss of the manuscripts, but on this evidence it seems
that the original versions of the other late novels, *Mansfield*

---

[1] William Gifford, reader to John Murray, wrote to the publisher on
29 September 1815: 'Of Emma, I have nothing but good to say. I was sure
of the writer before you mentioned her. The MS. though plainly written,
has yet some, indeed many little omissions; and an expression may now and
then be amended in passing through the press. I will readily undertake
the revision' (Samuel Smiles, *A Publisher and His Friends* (1891), i. 282).
It is unlikely that Jane Austen would have welcomed or adopted Gifford's
additions or amendments, but the posthumous edition of *Northanger Abbey*
and *Persuasion* may have been liable to such interference.

Park and *Emma*, would not be startlingly different from the texts that reached print.

NOTE

One other late change was made to *Persuasion*, the addition of the present chapter 10 in the second volume, an alteration which falls outside the scope of this study, but which I mention briefly as it concerns an adjustment made to the story in order to prepare for the two rewritten chapters. In the original design, as we can see from the opening of the manuscript chapter 10, Anne's reunion with Wentworth followed directly after her meeting with Mrs. Smith (the present chapter 9). In rewriting the manuscript chapters Jane Austen was probably struck by the similarities between chapters 9 and 11 (which were then consecutive). There is a repetition of design and method in the passages of revelation through dialogue. Moreover, Mrs. Smith's story gives us some new and rather surprising information, raising speculations which would tend to detract from the dramatic force of the reunion. The danger of a clash in interest was avoided by placing chapter 10 between these episodes, separating them temporally by a day, and by a variety of action and information: the comedy of the Elliot snobbery, the mystery of Mrs. Clay's connexion with Walter Elliot, and a further meeting between Anne and Wentworth, which serves to concentrate our attention upon the two central figures, and heightens the expectation with which we begin the following chapter.

7

THE LAST WORK, *SANDITON*

(1)

JANE Austen's emergence as a popular author dates from 1833, when a cheap edition of her works appeared in Bentley's library of Standard Novels. Within a few years her reputation rose sharply, largely through the efforts of one or two influential critics. In the *Edinburgh Review* for January 1843 Macaulay described her as a writer whose character-drawing 'approached nearest to the manner of the great master'[1] —Shakespeare himself. Five years later, reviewing a batch of novels for *Fraser's Magazine*,[2] George Henry Lewes linked Jane Austen's name with that of Fielding; these, he declared, were the greatest of English novelists; and like Macaulay, he also mentioned the name of Shakespeare. Charlotte Brontë, for one, was intrigued by these comparisons. Her own first novel, *Jane Eyre*, had been commended by Lewes, and writing to thank him, she took the opportunity to challenge his opinion of Jane Austen. Following his review in *Fraser's* she had turned to *Pride and Prejudice* with considerable expectation.

And what did I find? An accurate daguerreotyped portrait of a commonplace face;[3] a carefully fenced, highly cultivated garden, with neat borders and delicate flowers; but no glance of bright vivid physiognomy, no open country, no fresh air, no blue hill, no bonny beck. I should hardly like to live with her ladies and gentlemen, in their elegant but confined houses.[4]

George Sand she thought 'sagacious and profound'; Jane Austen

[1] Vol. lxxvi, p. 561: an anonymous article on Mme D'Arblay.
[2] Vol. xxxvi (December 1847), pp. 686–95.
[3] The portraits of Elizabeth Bennet on and facing the engraved title-page of Bentley's edition are indisputably 'commonplace'.
[4] Letter of 12 January 1848 (*The Brontës: Lives and Correspondence* (1932), ii. 179–80).

she found 'only shrewd and observant'.[1] In reply, Lewes insisted
that although Jane Austen was 'not a poetess', and lacked 'the
ravishing enthusiasm of poetry', she must none the less be
acknowledged as 'one of the greatest artists, of the greatest pain-
ters of human character'.[2] Charlotte Brontë met this claim with
a single question: 'Can there be a great artist without poetry?'[3]
Had she read one of the later novels, her opinion of Jane Austen
might have been different. In *Mansfield Park* and *Persuasion*
she could have found what she so admired in George Sand;
in *Emma* she could have enjoyed the 'open country', the 'fresh
air', and an escape from the 'elegant but confined houses'. Her
ultimate demand, however, was for 'poetry', and that quality
of imaginative writing she could have discovered above all in
Jane Austen's last, uncompleted work, the manuscript fragment *Sanditon*.

The opening chapters to this seventh novel herald an entirely new phase in Jane Austen's development. But in an early
and influential review[4] Mr. E. M. Forster makes no suggestion
that this is a work of such promise. He recognizes new features
in the presentation of scene and place, but dismisses the fragment as 'of small literary merit', judging that 'the numerous
alterations in the MS. are never in the direction of vitality'; that
'so far as character-drawing is concerned, Jane Austen is here
completely in the grip of her previous novels'; and that it 'gives
the effect of weakness, if only because it is reminiscent from
first to last'. The circumstances of her life at that time certainly
give colour to Mr. Forster's remarks. When Jane Austen wrote
Sanditon she was seriously ill, and one might well suppose that
bodily fatigue would bring with it the kind of creative weakness
that Mr. Forster detects.

From dates on the manuscript we know that Jane Austen
began the story on 17 January 1817, her last illness already far
advanced. Having written and revised about 24,000 words, she

---

[1] Ibid., p. 180.
[2] Quoted by Charlotte Brontë in letter of 12 January 1848, ibid. [3] Ibid.
[4] *The Nation*, 21 March 1925, p. 860, reprinted in *Abinger Harvest* (1936),
p. 14 .

abandoned the novel on 18 March, exactly four months before her death. Its composition may have been a race against time. The decline in health, which she did her best to conceal, had been noticeable as far back as March 1816, when she had already been at work on *Persuasion* for eight months. Caroline Austen recalls that 'Aunt Jane's health began to fail some time before we knew she was really ill'.[1] A year later her condition had deteriorated; *Northanger Abbey* was laid aside, and *Persuasion* may not have been revised to her complete satisfaction. Although, as James Austen-Leigh relates, she 'continued to work at it as long as she could work at all',[2] the final stages of illness compelled her to abandon *Sanditon* after only two months' writing. Four months later, on 18 July 1817, she died.

Yet far from betraying the author's physical condition, as Mr. Forster's review would suggest, *Sanditon* is the most vigorous of all Jane Austen's writing. There is not the least sign of fatigue in its style, invention, or design. It reveals the author responding as never before to the world around her—to the landscape and sun—and answering the spirit of the age, the current of Romantic sensibility, catching something of its buoyancy and zest. At the same time she holds an ironic and critical stance towards both Romanticism and the social ethos of Regency England. The follies of literary enthusiasm, business speculation and hypochondria are treated no less sharply than the cult of 'sentimental' sensibility which she had ridiculed many years before. And while the satire is often severe, there is no lack of tenderness and compassion, a remarkable intermingling of feeling and wit. With this widened subject-matter and a fuller response to the energy and beauty of nature there comes an enrichment of her descriptive and narrative prose. The neatness and formality of her accustomed style, a personal adjustment of Augustan tradition, is relaxed and varied with a new rhythmical freedom and a fresh use of language, notably in

---

[1] *My Aunt*, p. 13.
[2] Letter to Miss Quincey, 30 December 1870, quoted by M. A. Dewolfe Howe, 'A Jane Austen Letter', *Yale Review* (1926), N.S. xv. 335.

figurative and symbolic devices that we would call poetic. These
are developments for which there is little hint in the earlier
novels.

If in certain other respects we recognize the progress here
as an evolution of her practised art, this is not to agree with Mr.
Forster that *Sanditon* is 'reminiscent from first to last'. He com-
pares (among other details) the carriage accident at the opening
with that in 'Love and Friendship', the sprained ankles of Mr.
Parker and Marianne Dashwood, Arthur's trust in cocoa with
Mr. Woodhouse's faith in gruel. This list of incidental resemblances can be extended. Other characters, topics, and
events in *Sanditon* can be isolated in this way in order to further an argument that the work is 'reminiscent'. But the points
of similarity are superficial and commonplace; if *Sanditon* is at
all reminiscent, it is so in directions more subtle and important
than Mr. Forster suggests.

The strongest association with the past is in the continuing
vein of broad comic fun and literary satire that dominates much
of the juvenilia, reappears more moderately in *Sense and Sensibility* and *Northanger Abbey*, and is now revived in the eccentricities of the Parker family and Sir Edward Denham. In her
earliest writing Jane Austen was able to put the fanciful promp-
tings of her childhood imagination to the service of burlesque;
later, in her mature writing, this playfulness takes a different
expression, such as we find in her drawing of the countryside
behind Lyme, 'with its green chasms between romantic rocks',[1]
and in this picture of Anne:

> Prettier musings of high-wrought love and eternal constancy,
> could never have passed along the streets of Bath, than Anne was
> sporting with from Camden-place to Westgate-buildings. It was almost
> enough to spread purification and perfume all the way.[2]

Such figurative language is rare in the novels. There is also a
hint of poetry, beyond formal analysis, in the description of
Anne's and Wentworth's stroll along the gravel walk. At these
points there is a breath of the imaginative power that runs

[1] p. 95.   [2] p. 192.

throughout every part of *Sanditon*. The delicate expression of mood and atmosphere is also matched in both works by the sharpness of the satire, directed against Sir Walter and his eldest daughter in *Persuasion*, and in *Sanditon* against invalidism and seaside resorts, topics glanced at lightly in *Persuasion* and *Emma*. To this limited extent we can relate *Sanditon* to the earlier writing.

It is more profitable to discuss *Sanditon* in terms of its obvious originality, the immediately striking feature being the treatment of place. The village has an importance far beyond that of any location in the earlier novels. It is not simply a gathering-ground for the characters (as, for example, Jane Austen had used London and Bath); nor is it merely an appropriate setting (as Lyme is a home for the naval families, and a place to which an excursion might conveniently be made). It possesses something we find nowhere else in Jane Austen— a distinctive *genius loci*, created through its topography, its atmosphere of wind and sun, its social climate, its population, and its way of life. The prominence and significance of the setting, in the design and effect of the story, is clearly a departure from her conventional methods, and it accompanies a change in the scope of her subject-matter. The shift in emphasis is from the individual in society to society itself.

In taking this setting—the neighbourhood of a fishing village-cum-coastal resort—Jane Austen was choosing a location which epitomized certain dominant features of contemporary middle-class life, namely, its expansion, its restlessness, its pursuit of pleasure and elegance, its materialism, and its immorality. There was ample precedent for this view of the seaside. In 1775 Langhorne had described Brighthelmstone, already the most popular resort, as the favoured haunt of the 'modern Man of Fashion'.[1] A few years later Cowper wrote more scathingly of a society so 'Ingenious to diversify dull life' that 'all, impatient of dry land agree With one consent, to rush into the sea'.[2] In the popular

---

[1] *The Country Justice* (1775), pt. ii, l. 148, and see ll. 152–63.
[2] *Retirement* (1782), from ll. 515–24.

mind Brighton was the home of fashionable extravagance and debauchery as drawn by Rowlandson an impression confirmed by the appearance of the 'wicked Pavillion' (as Mrs. Creevey described it to her husband)[1] and the court of the Prince Regent. As a child Jane Austen was aware of its notoriety; London and Brighton were Lady Lesley's 'favourite haunts of Dissipation'.[2] It was a spot Jane Austen was pleased to avoid, as she explained to Cassandra;[3] a place to set the downfall of Lydia Bennet, in whose imagination 'a visit to Brighton comprised every possibility of earthly happiness. She saw with the creative eye of fancy, the streets of that gay bathing place covered with officers.'[4] Elizabeth Bennet's disgust at this plan is matched, in *Emma*, by the distaste of Mr. Knightley, who associates such places with 'the idlest haunts in the kingdom',[5] a notoriety well-deserved, judging by the flood of scurrilous verse-satires which circulated about this time.[6] Perhaps it was the breath of scandal which offended Jane Austen at Weymouth in 1804, and led her to describe it to Cassandra as 'altogether a shocking place'.[7] It was not the sea she objected to, for she enjoyed the bathing.

In general Jane Austen's observation of seaside manners has a note of gaiety, not unlike the tone of Bloomfield's *News from Worthing*,[8] a gently satirical account of the poet's delight at the flirtatiousness of the visiting young ladies. In *Sanditon*, however, the satire is also directed far more acutely at what, in his age, Cowper had divined as the pursuit of novelty and pleasure,

---

[1] Letter of 29 October 1805, *The Creevey Papers* (1963), ed. John Gore, p. 54.

[2] *Volume the Second*, p. 89.

[3] *Letters*, p. 49, 8 January 1799: 'I assure you that I dread the idea of going to Brighton as much as you do, but I am not without hopes that something may happen to prevent it.'

[4] *Pride and Prejudice*, p. 232.   [5] *Emma*, p. 146.

[6] For example, see *The Balnea* (1801), by George Sackville Carey; *Royal Rantipoles or the Humours of Brighton* (1815), by Peter Pindar; and other works cited by Osbert Sitwell and Margaret Barton, *Brighton* (1935).

[7] *Letters*, p. 139.

[8] I can find no date for this poem. Mr. D. J. Davis points out to me that in the 'Advertisement to the Reader' prefaced to *Hazlewood Hall* (1823) Bloomfield refers (p. iii) to a visit to Worthing in 1805.

and what Jane Austen sensed as an uneasy spirit of change. Her story is full of migrant figures, of visitors in search of health, profit, or fashionable company. As Hazlitt was to observe, 'People at a watering-place may be compared to the flies of a summer'.[1] Sanditon, too, has its share of 'gads'. Landowners are tempted by the visions of development. The traditional ways of life in the country families and the village are upset by a newly awakened concern for fashion and profit.

This aspect of Sanditon is communicated briskly and wittily in chapter 4, which describes Charlotte Heywood's arrival with Mr. and Mrs. Parker. Jane Austen differentiates among the three parts of the village. First, there is

the Church and real[2] village of Sanditon, which stood at the foot of the Hill. . . . The Village contained little more than Cottages, but the Spirit of the day had been caught, as Mr. P. observed with delight to Charlotte, & two or three of the best of them were smartened up with a white Curtain & 'Lodgings to let'—, and farther on, in the little Green Court of an old Farm House, two Females in elegant white were actually to be seen with their books & camp stools—and in turning the corner of the Baker's shop, the sound of a Harp might be heard through the upper Casement.[3]

When they pass the shoemaker's window Mr. Parker bursts out, 'Civilization, Civilization indeed! . . . Blue Shoes, & nankin Boots! Who wd have expected such a sight at a Shoemaker's in old Sanditon!'[4] On the Hill 'Modern'[5] Sanditon begins, with its

one short row of smart-looking Houses, called the Terrace, with a broad walk in front, aspiring to be the Mall of the Place. In this row were the best Milliner's shop & the Library—a little detached from it, the Hotel & Billiard Room—Here began the Descent to the Beach, and to the Bathing Machines—& this was therefore the favourite spot for Beauty & Fashion.[6]

[1] *Notes of a Journey Through France and Italy* (1826), p. 4. Hazlitt is referring specifically to seaside resorts.
[2] p. 51 (Chapman reads 'neat', but Jane Austen appears to have written 'real'). The manuscript is revised at this point. Jane Austen originally wrote 'The Church & village of original Sanditon'. The revision effects an evaluative comparison between the old part and the new residential quarter on the Hill.   [3] pp. 51–52.   [4] p. 53.
[5] p. 54.   [6] p. 55.

The only part of the village untouched by 'the Spirit of the day' is 'a 3d Habitable Division, in a small cluster of Fisherman's Houses'.[1]

This little backwater is a paradigm of the larger world. In it is figured the malaise of the times, what Cobbett diagnosed as its 'morbid restlessness', expressed in the growth of towns such as Brighton:

a place of no trade; of no commerce at all; it has no harbour; it is no place of deposit or of transit for corn or for goods or for cattle . . . the valleys and sides of hills, now covered with elegant houses, were formerly corn-fields, and downs for the pasture of sheep. Very pretty is the town and its virandas, and carriages, and harnessed goats; very pretty to *behold*; but dismal to think of. . . .[2]

This is the verdict of the radical agrarian economist. For Jane Austen too, the growth of Sanditon is fraught with consequence, which as a novelist she renders and interprets obliquely through the work of art, without formal analysis. For her, then, Sanditon is not simply the setting for a story, but a phenomenon both of nature and contemporary life, the expression of a social ethos whose influence is pervasive, stimulating, and dangerous.

But no interpretation or description of this work can safely be developed unless we keep in mind that the manuscript is a first draft. Dr. Chapman believes that 'a certain roughness and harshness of satire . . . which at its worst amounts to caricature'[3] would have been reduced in final revision. Working against time Jane Austen may have been trying to write herself in, feeling her way as quickly and emphatically as possible, and perhaps at this time of sickness, not as surely as usual. We must consider to what extent the completed and revised novel, or a draft written under more leisurely circumstances, would differ from the fragment. To ignore this would be to run the danger of taking some temporary feature in the work's evolution (which revision would

---

[1] p. 51.
[2] *Rural Rides*, ed. G. D. H. and M. Cole (1930), i. 690–1, entry for 5 May 1823.
[3] *Facts and Problems*, p. 208.

modify or remove) for a new style and method of treatment. The expression in many passages is so energetic and elliptical that judged beside the earlier novels it wears the look of haste, as if Jane Austen were roughing out the main lines of a character or description as she went along, intending to develop it later—for example, this description of Mr. Parker:

> Upon the whole, Mr. P. was evidently an amiable, family-man, fond of Wife, Childn, Brothers & Sisters—& generally kind-hearted; —Liberal, gentlemanlike, easy to please;—of a sanguine turn of mind, with more Imagination than Judgement.[1]

If we regard this sentence as a quick listing of traits to be expanded, as notes for a fuller treatment, we should expect much of its briskness and concentration to disappear in revision. However, the effect of the alterations to the manuscript is in the opposite direction; there is no sign of expansion or formalization; the changes are to strengthen the characteristic vigour and economy. There is no evidence that Jane Austen was modifying her treatment, as she was, for example, in the manuscript chapter 11 of *Persuasion*, or in Lord Osborne's meeting with Emma Watson.[2] The very next sentence supports this contention. Its perfectly balanced rhythm and fully expanded structure, its formality, polish, and delicately judged irony, typical features of her developed style in the mature novels, are achieved with the correction of a single word:

> And Mrs. P. was as evidently a gentle, amiable, sweet tempered Woman, the properest wife in the World for a Man of strong Understanding, but not of capacity to supply the cooler reflection which her own Husband sometimes needed, & so entirely waiting to be guided on every occasion, that whether he were risking his Fortune or spraining his Ancle, she remained equally useless.[3]

(*was* to *remained*[4] is the only change.) The preceding sentence is staccato and explosive, the energy and gusto carrying the essence of Mr. Parker's manner and speech. It is as deliberately contrived as the following sentence, where the formalization of

---

[1] p. 23.   [2] See above, pp. 75–76.
[3] pp. 23–24.   [4] p. 24, note to l. 2.

style denotes a shift in the point of view, now permitting the author's descriptive commentary to proceed with its own especial ironic tone. Such abrupt and extreme changes in style are to be found throughout the work, not as a consequence of failing powers or haste, but as only one of the means, though very prominent, of communicating the tempo of life in which these characters exist, and which they create for themselves in their excitement and activity. Jane Austen is not sketching a story, but producing a draft which only requires continuation and the revision of minor details (such as the expansion of abbreviations, and paragraphing) to reach a final state.

(11)

If, then, we judge that the corrected and revised first draft goes a considerable way towards fulfilling the author's intention, our opinion of the fragment, with regard to its literary importance and its place in Jane Austen's development, can be reached with some assurance. There is, however, a difficulty of interpretation which does not arise in the case of the earlier novel fragment, *The Watsons*. That piece, about 6,000 words shorter than *Sanditon*, seems (in Miss Lascelles' phrase) 'almost to foreshadow its own fulfilment',[1] and there is a continuation to tell us the future history of the characters and plot. The opening establishes the social context in which the story is to proceed; we are given accurate information about the principal figures and their relationships to one another. With some refinements this is the method employed for each of the novels. The values, and behaviour of the individuals, and the social structure are conventional and regular; the exceptions are soon pointed out and remain unmistakable. But *Sanditon* does not conform to this pattern, and in examining its leading characteristics I hope to show that the many puzzles of detail and the general uncertainty about the direction of the plot are not signs of confusion or incoherence on Jane Austen's part, but intended features of

[1] *Jane Austen*, p. 39.

the design which would be essential to the meaning of the completed work.[1]

From the opening—the account of an accident involving a 'Gentleman & Lady',[2] unnamed for eleven pages—we become increasingly aware of the novelty of Jane Austen's subject-matter and treatment. There is little to remind us of the familiar order, the way of life in which her other stories are established. The new community is at an awkward age of growth. The leading figures are eccentrics. Only the Misses Beaufort are represented, ironically, as typical and commonplace: they are 'just such young ladies as may be met with, in at least one family out of three, throughout the Kingdom'.[3] Mr. Parker, Diana, Arthur, and Sir Edward are idiosyncratic, Dickensian figures, their conversation and behaviour dominated by some wild, leading passion. These four figures constitute a small gallery of human absurdity, types that we usually find at the edge of Jane Austen's world, in the Palmers, Miss Bates, Mr. Collins, and Mr. Yates, minor eccentrics now expanded to take the centre of the stage. There is no sacrifice of realism here. These broader, more emphatic figures take their part in a more emphatic and broadly drawn setting; the scale and force of Jane Austen's effects are adjusted to match them. Part of this achievement is to make the improbable of life probable in fiction. It has been remarked that figures as wild and strange as Sir Edward and Diana Parker could be met;[4] and indeed, Jane Austen herself knew a Diana Parker in Mrs. Edward Bridges, wife of the Rector of Lenham. In September 1813 the Bridges called at Godmersham Park (the country seat of Edward

---

[1] We can assume that such a total meaning did exist in Jane Austen's mind, if not on paper. *The Watsons* was planned to its conclusion; and there is no reason to doubt that *Sanditon* too was fully planned.   [2] p. 1.
[3] p. 152.
[4] C. J. Rawson points to Fanny Burney's encounter with a man whose eccentricities are exactly those of Sir Edward ('The Sentimental Hero in Fiction and Life: A Note on Jane Austen and Fanny Burney', *Notes and Queries*, cciii (1958), 253–4). M. H. Dodds draws attention to a woman similar to Diana Parker ('Captain Charles Austen and Some Others', Section iii, *Notes and Queries*, cxcii (1947), 274–5).

Knight), now on their way home after a summer passed at
Ramsgate 'for *her* health, she is a poor Honey—the sort of
woman who gives me the idea of being determined never to be
well—& who likes her spasms & nervousness & the consequence they give her, better than anything else.'[1]

Slightly apart from the eccentrics are the more familiar types
of Jane Austen's world: Charlotte Heywood,[2] the quiet, perceptive, observing heroine of twenty-two; the slightly mysterious
Clara Brereton, perhaps her rival; and Sidney Parker, the witty,
fashionable young man, possibly to emerge as the hero, or an
adventurer. These three look coolly and critically upon the
enthusiasms of their companions. Between these extremes stands
Lady Denham, the most complex figure, a woman of shrewdness and cunning, whose calculation is concealed beneath a
display of petty foibles.

The society in which these characters are placed is far more
extensive than that we find elsewhere in Jane Austen's writing.
We are made aware of a working neighbourhood (a foil to the
leisurely and moneyed visitors), and of relationships between
the classes. We learn something of the lives of the servants
and tradesmen, especially as they are touched by Mr. Parker's
venture: his butler, Lady Denham's gardener, from whom he
buys vegetables, old Stringer and his son, whom he has encouraged to set up as market-gardeners, old Andrew, his own gardener, William Heeley, the shoemaker, Jebb's, the milliners,
and Whitby's, the subscription library and general shop. To
this extent Jane Austen's fictional scene was widening to
include the day-to-day concerns of people outside the conventional middle-class family groups, until now the staple
population of her works.

As the opening section of a full-scale work, this fragment is

---

[1] *Letters*, p. 339.

[2] In a letter to Cassandra, 11 October 1813, Jane Austen wrote: 'I admire
the Sagacity & Taste of Charlotte Williams. Those large dark eyes always
judge well.—I will compliment her, by naming a Heroine after her' (*Letters*,
p. 345). Perhaps Charlotte Heywood is this compliment; they have more
than a name in common.

strikingly different from the equivalent parts of the other novels. Far from establishing the groundwork of the action and setting the figures in their typical and defining patterns of behaviour, it breeds an air of mystery. The future of the story remains uncertain. According to a family tradition passed down from Francis, Jane Austen intended the work to be known not as *Sanditon* (a title given by the family[1]) but as 'The Brothers'.[2] Is this title itself deliberately misleading? Or are Thomas, Sidney, and Arthur, really to dominate the story, or to provide structural centres for the plotting? As the work stands, it is difficult to imagine how this could be done. Does Jane Austen plan to subordinate the conventional social drives of money and marriage to the new economic force of land speculation? What importance is to be given to the satire on hypochondria? Are the eccentrics to lead the plot, or will the more serious characters take control? What is to be disclosed about Clara, Esther, and Lady Denham? Are the Heywood family to re-enter the story? What is the emotional centre of the work to be? Charlotte Heywood appears to be cast for the role of heroine, but Jane Austen has not attempted to direct our sympathy towards her. The centre of interest is outside—in Sanditon, and the several groups of figures. These questions cannot be answered; they occur as one of the outstanding features of our response; they are the outcome of a deliberate and meaningful enigma in almost every aspect of the story.

Each stage of the work is dominated by one of the strongly drawn figures—Mr. Parker, Diana, Arthur, Sir Edward, and Lady Denham—the passages being linked by Charlotte's experience as the point of view through which much of the action is observed. In this respect *Sanditon* can be described as a novel of characters, while the action and setting can be interpreted in terms of anti-romance, a burlesque on the melodrama of popular fiction. The initial catastrophe is nothing more

---

[1] *Life*, p. 381 n. On what authority this title was given we are not told.

[2] Revealed by Mrs. J. Sanders (a grand-daughter of Francis) in a letter to *The Times Literary Supplement* (19 February 1925, p. 120); Dr. Chapman adds to this information, *Minor Works*, p. 363 n.

than an overturned carriage and a sprained ankle; the scene of the accident, a spot no wilder than farmland in the Sussex Downs; the traveller's quest, a surgeon; the excitement centres upon a business speculation; a mock-Lovelace intent on seducing a victim who is in not the least danger of falling; while the inheritance motif—a rich, tyrannical old lady, courted for her fortune, and accompanied by a dependent young woman in distressed circumstances—is treated with comic irony. Most of the action is played out in the light and security of an English watering-place, Jane Austen's burlesque antithesis to the gloomy terrors of a Gothic stronghold.

The sustained and explicit literary satire is developed through detailed observation of a specific middle-class group, now fired by 'a spirit of restless activity'[1] (as Charlotte reflects on the Parkers). The conventional preoccupations with money, rank, and marriage are thrown into sharp relief in this new world, which has yet to settle its code of manners. All is movement and change: in the heroine's shifting impressions, in the arrival of visitors, in the village itself. There is an emphatic contrast between the settled, traditional past, the instability of the present, and uncertainty about the future. This contrast, made throughout the work, is figured initially between Mr. Parker and Mr. Heywood. The cautious and conservative gentleman-farmer has been content to pass his fifty-seven years tucked away at Willingden. He and his wife are now 'older in Habits than in Age'.[2] The bringing up of their large family has kept them to 'a very quiet, settled, careful course of Life'.[3] Mr. Heywood's only thought for Sanditon is that its development will raise 'the price of Provisions & make the Poor good for nothing—'.[4] He is a staunch reactionary, not simply in comic opposition to Mr. Parker, but as a man who has enjoyed a long and happy seclusion with his family. He speaks for a way of life, as well as out of prejudice.

Mr. Parker is also a devoted family man, but he puts his trust in the future of Sanditon, a progress that involves him in a break

[1] p. 130.   [2] p. 26.   [3] p. 27.   [4] p. 13.

with the past. In answer to Charlotte's inquiry (as they approach Sanditon), 'And whose very snug-looking place is this?', Mr. Parker replies,

> This is my old House—the house of my Forefathers—the house where I & all my Brothers & Sisters were born and bred—& where my own 3 eldest Children were born—where Mrs. P. & I lived till within the last 2 years—till our new House was finished.—I am glad you are pleased with it.—It is an honest old Place.[1]

For a moment he is overcome by affection and regret, but when his wife also speaks fondly of their old home he comforts her with the assurance that at Trafalgar House they can enjoy 'all the Grandeur of the Storm, with less real danger'.[2] Thus Mr. Parker is able to reconcile Romanticism with prudence. He turns his back upon the past, and changes the pattern of his life to meet the fashions of the time. In this he is a striking portrait of a new social phenomenon—the member of the landed gentry who capitalizes his property and goes into business with the kind of rash enthusiasm and innocent lack of principle that the amateur in commerce so often shows.

His partner, the elderly Lady Denham, is the traditional shrewd and wealthy widow who plays off one hopeful beneficiary against another. She too seeks to profit from the development of Sanditon. Her wits have already won her a fortune and a title, and she views ill health, this new source of wealth, with cynical avarice. Much of her conversation is in the jargon of economics, and is filled with references to 'Income ... Property, Landed or Funded ... Heiresses ... Half pay officers ... Widows with only a Jointure'.[3] Like Mr. Heywood she is fearful of the effect of bringing doctors to Sanditon: 'It wd be only encouraging our Servants & the Poor to fancy themselves ill.'[4]

Her nephew, Sir Edward, is the familiar rake, now adjusted to *Sanditon* as a Regency Lovelace, a buffoon affecting an extravagant literary Romanticism, his small mind burdened with choice passages from Montgomery, Campbell, Wordsworth,

[1] pp. 43–44.   [2] p. 48.
[3] pp. 99–100.   [4] pp. 80–81.

Scott, and Burns. His reading convinces him that 'the soul of
high toned Genius. . . . The Coruscations of Talent, elicited
by impassioned feeling in the breast of Man, are perhaps in-
compatible with some of the prosaic Decencies of Life.'[1] As
she had mocked the doctrine of sensibility Jane Austen now
ridicules the libertarian notions of Romanticism, or at least those
notions as voiced by an impressionable young enthusiast.
Charlotte's response to these wild ideas is primly correct. She
confesses that 'Burns's known Irregularities, greatly interrupt
my enjoyment of his Lines';[2] and on Sir Edward's argument
for artistic freedom she reflects 'This was very fine;—but if
Charlotte understood it at all, not very moral—.'[3] The clash
here, as between Mr. Parker and Mr. Heywood, is between the
old and the new: the old perhaps a trifle narrow, over-decorous,
and timid, but with the virtues of restraint and common sense;
the new full of energy and infectious enthusiasm, but so often
rash and blind. Between these extremes is Lady Denham, who
uses a life's experience to exploit the present, associating herself
with Mr. Parker's schemes on the calculation of profit. Thus
Jane Austen makes no simple judgement upon the age. The
weaknesses and qualities of past and present are held in an
active and critical relationship. Change is upon Sanditon, upon
its visitors and inhabitants, upon their ideas and their way of life,
perfect material for the comedy of manners. More profoundly,
Jane Austen was fascinated by the process of change itself, in
the energy and activity which it displays. It is this which pro-
vokes in her such a complex and fruitful response.

The theme figured through these characters, setting, and
events, can be sufficiently indicated if we give *Sanditon* the
sub-title 'Delusion and Reality'. It is true, of course, that Jane
Austen's writing is, as a whole, concerned more or less explicitly
with drawing the distinction between appearance and reality.
But in *Sanditon* the prominence of this theme is comparable with
the ethical topics—sense and sensibility, pride and prejudice,
and persuasion—indicated by the titles of the three earlier novels.

[1] pp. 92–93.   [2] p. 92.   [3] p. 93.

Throughout this fragment the varieties of illusion, or deluded vision, enlightenment, and undeluded vision, are illustrated in two ways: firstly, through the mental experience of the characters, and secondly, through Jane Austen's method of referring to these figures to remind us that they are not autonomous or historical beings, but creations, playing their parts in a fiction.

The first method is employed from the opening of the work, where Mr. Parker's reading of facts and circumstances is almost always falsified by his humour, an incurable optimism which leads him to hold stubbornly to his eccentric point of view. He takes the lane in defiance of the coachman's warning; congratulates himself on escaping free from injury, only to find he has a sprained ankle; believes he is fit to continue his journey at once, and has to stay at Willingdon two weeks; assumes that a neighbouring cottage, which turns out to be a labourer's home, must be the surgeon's house; and insists at length, against Mr. Heywood's certain knowledge, that there is a surgeon in the neighbourhood. More generally, his life is dedicated to a bubble speculation for which he conceives no possibility of failure. Jane Austen's audience would have shared Mr. Heywood's scepticism about this enterprise; his comment is a timely warning:

Every five years, one hears of some new place or other starting up by the Sea, & growing the fashion.—How they can half of them be filled, is the wonder![1]

In contrast to his guest Mr. Heywood is a man of rational and conservative sense. He curbs the flow of Mr. Parker's optimism, correcting or opposing his misinterpretation of facts and wildness of opinion. The contrast between delusion and reality is established in these two figures; the clash of views is clear and emphatic, and in the course of the work this theme is developed more subtly in situations of increasing complexity.

After the first two chapters, with Mr. Parker at Willingden, the main theme is linked to the education of the heroine's judgement: Charlotte is to learn the extent to which his view of other

[1] p. 12.

people is coloured by optimism and blind trust. During the
drive to Sanditon he describes those she is to meet: Lady
Denham, Clara, Sir Edward, Esther, Sidney, and later, Arthur,
and his two sisters. There is, as we see later, a wide discrepancy
between Mr. Parker's view and the judgement Charlotte forms
on meeting these people: in almost every case experience leads
her to a contrary opinion. She has also to learn that her own
first impressions are not infallible. 'sober-minded'[1] and observing the world 'with the calmness of amused Curiosity',[2] she is
not immediately proof against Sir Edward's flattering attentions.
She accepts him as a pleasing companion, and the truth dawns
only when she observes his interest in Clara, a revelation

which altogether gave an hasty turn to Charlotte's fancy, cured her
of her halfhour's fever, & placed her in a more capable state of judging, when Sir Edw: was gone, of *how* agreable he had actually been.[3]

Mr. Parker assured her of his brother's and sisters' ill health;
there is, he insists, 'No chance of seeing them at Sanditon';[4]
but they arrive, and she finds Diana an active organizer. Having
fancied Arthur 'a very puny, delicate-looking young Man', she
'was astonished to find him quite as tall as his Brother & a
great deal Stouter—Broad made & Lusty'.[5] It is in their estimates
of Lady Denham that Mr. Parker and Charlotte are most widely
at variance. Charlotte's immediate impressions are favourable.
Although she notes 'a shrewd eye, & self-satisfied air', an abrupt,
outspoken manner, she judges that there is 'a good humour &
cordiality about her'.[6] After some conversation, however, this
opinion is reversed. She is convinced that Lady Denham

is thoroughly mean. I had not expected any thing so bad.—Mr. P.
spoke too mildly of her.—His Judgement is evidently not to be
trusted.—His own Good nature misleads him. He is too kind hearted
to see clearly.—I must judge for myself. . . . But she is very, very
mean.—I can see no Good in her.[7]

The contradiction of Mr. Parker's judgement and the reversal
of her own first impression is violent, and it may be that later

[1] p. 76.   [2] p. 54.   [3] p. 86.   [4] p. 59.
[5] p. 133.   [6] p. 74.   [7] pp. 103–4.

Jane Austen intended to modify Charlotte's views again, to give her a more temperate opinion.

Lady Denham is the decisive test of the heroine's perception. Charlotte bases her view of the older woman on the long conversation in which Lady Denham discusses her life with an air of frankness.[1] But her manner is calculated, the revelation is aimed at controlling the girl's opinion of Sir Edward, Esther, and herself, rather than at making any real confidences. She claims to be a person 'not very easily taken-in',[2] and remarks later, 'I always take care to know what I am about & who I have to deal with, before I stir a finger'.[3] Lady Denham—so shrewd and suspicious, seeking continually for hidden motives, anticipating deceit—was perhaps to get no nearer to the truth than Mr. Parker, who thinks well of everyone. Her self-assurance may be as ill-fated as that of Diana, who would 'be anything rather than not clear',[4] but whose schemes end in comic confusion.

Clara Brereton is another test for Charlotte's judgement. Like the heroine, she is perceptive; she sees through Sir Edward (no difficult task), and popular opinion has it that she is strong-minded, a woman of influence, 'the very companion who wd guide & soften Lady D—who wd enlarge her mind & open her hand'.[5] So when Mr. Parker, who is so often wrong, introduces her as a paragon,[6] and Charlotte, whose first impressions are sometimes faulty, identifies her with 'the idea of a complete Heroine',[7] we suspect that a hidden character is yet to be revealed in Clara. When the fragment ends, after Charlotte's glimpse of Clara in the grounds of Sanditon House, the heroine has still far to go in the penetration of the other woman's motives and behaviour.

Sidney was probably to have been the third main challenge to her judgement. A gifted young man, as Mr. Parker tells Charlotte, he is 'privileged by superior abilities or spirits to say anything'.[8] He regards the Sanditon project as nothing more than a joke,[9] and shares Charlotte's understanding that there is a 'good deal of Imagination'[10] in the complaints of his

[1] pp. 94–102.   [2] p. 95.   [3] p. 96.   [4] p. 120.   [5] p. 42.
[6] pp. 41–42.   [7] p. 75.   [8] p. 50.   [9] Ibid.   [10] p. 58.

hypochondriac sisters. Little as we know of him and Clara, it seems likely that they were to join the heroine, and perhaps Lady Denham, to form a group around whom the more serious aspects of the story were to develop, slightly apart from the literary satire and the comedy of the eccentrics.

The discrimination between reality and appearance is not always an easy matter, even for the perceptive, sensible, and level-headed such as Charlotte. The relationship between Lady Denham and her niece is open to speculation. As Jane Austen remarks, the difference between the proud and silent Miss Denham in company, and the warmth and vivacity she displays when alone with Lady Denham, 'was very striking—and very amusing—or very melancholy, just as Satire or Morality might prevail'.[1] Having observed this ambiguity Jane Austen at once records that 'Miss Denham's Character was pretty well decided with Charlotte'.[2] Clearly, Charlotte is unwise to be so decisive in her judgement, for her own experience of the world is limited, and the possibilities of interpretation are wide. Even Mr. Parker, usually so opinionated and decisive, recognizes that on occasion there must be qualification and tentativeness. After describing Lady Denham to Charlotte he remarks, uncharacteristically, 'Those who tell their own Story you know must be listened to with Caution.—When you see us in contact, you will judge for yourself.'[3] Coming from him, this is warning indeed.

The circumstances that can make the apprehension of truth a delicate process are suggested again, and in a very different way, at the close of the fragment, when Charlotte, Mrs. Parker, and Mary set out for Sanditon House.

It was a close, misty morng, & when they reached the brow of the Hill, they could not for some time make out what sort of Carriage it was, which they saw coming up. It appeared at different moments to be everything from the Gig to the Pheaton,—from one horse to 4.[4]

The traveller is Sidney, who may turn out to be a candidate for Charlotte's hand, or, if not her eventual husband, at least someone deeply involved in her future. His entry to the story (like

[1] p. 87.   [2] p. 88.   [3] p. 35.   [4] p. 164.

the first glimpse of Mr. Howard at the assembly in *The Watsons*) is a moment of importance, and the uncertainty about his carriage, the deceptiveness of the visual impression, is a descriptive element which I believe Jane Austen is using in order to figure some enigmatic quality about Sidney himself. Perhaps he is a deceiver; perhaps Charlotte is not to understand him so rapidly as she has penetrated the others. (Is this kind of symbolic action, or prefigurement, also used at the opening? Impetuosity brings Mr. Parker to a literal fall. Does this portend another catastrophe? Will enthusiasm lead him to the failure of his seaside speculations?) Immediately after the meeting with Sidney the three women continue their walk towards Sanditon House, and Jane Austen describes with a curious particularity the exact relationship between the winding road, its fence, the bordering trees, and the fence beyond. In this clear-cut scene Charlotte

caught a glimpse over the pales of something White & Womanish in the field on the other side;—it was a something which immediately brought Miss B. into her head—& stepping to the pales, she saw indeed—& very decidedly, in spite of the Mist. . . .[1]

She reflects on 'the extreme difficulty which secret Lovers must have in finding a proper spot for their stolen Interveiws'.[2] As Dr. Chapman remarks, 'All the items of *chiaroscurc*—the mist, the treacherous fence, the ill-defined flutter of ribbons—add up to an effect which is as clearly deliberate as it is certainly novel'.[3] The contrast is between the certainty of external facts (the precise relationship of the road, the fence, the trees, and grounds, to one another), the visual impression, which is both vague and detailed, and the mental impression, Charlotte's interpretation of the scene according to her preconceptions about Clara and Sir Edward. What significance this would have in the finished work is, of course, uncertain; possibly it would be as important as the description of the movements of the visitors about the grounds of Sotherton, with the same kind of symbolic value;

[1] p. 167.   [2] p. 169.   [3] *Facts and Problems*, p. 209.

but its connexion with the main theme is evident. Charlotte is presented with a major test of judgement. The connexion between Sir Edward and Clara is as ambiguous in some respects, as plain in others, as the details of the scene before her. The 'moralising reflection which the sight of this Tete a Tete produced'[1] (quoted above) is couched in a novelistic cliché diction and phraseology.[2] Charlotte's thoughts are remarkably generous and undisapproving; yet they flow readily into a conventional mould, just as they did on her first sight of Lady Denham and Clara,[3] and again, when she sees them a second time.[4] Jane Austen has already made the point that compared with Sir Edward Denham the girl's 'feelings were not the result of any spirit of Romance' and that 'she was a very sober-minded young Lady, sufficiently well-read in Novels to supply her Imagination with amusement, but not at all unreasonably influenced by them'.[5] Nevertheless, faced by this unfamiliar situation, for want of experience she relies unconsciously upon her reading in the formulation of her ideas. The course of the story might have shown a development in the heroine's already striking capacity to judge for herself, until she is able to escape completely from the modes of thinking that literature might induce. She has already discovered very quickly that her own impressions can be misleading; perhaps in the future her decisions are to be less categorical and reached with a cautiousness that the nature of reality, and her own past errors, will teach her to observe.

So far I have considered how the problem of distinguishing between illusion and reality is posed for the heroine in particular. I believe that this problem is also posed deliberately and externally for the reader; that Jane Austen is being purposely enigmatic, challenging us to fathom the importance of the characters and the direction of the plot. Mr. Parker, Diana, Sir Edward, and Lady Denham are revealed at length, but, with

---

[1] pp. 168–9.
[2] 'Tete a Tete' is one of Jane Austen's 'due scraps of Italian & French' (*Letters*, p. 135), and is used facetiously in the letters, see pp. 84, 131, 188, 200, 240, 335.
[3] pp. 75–76.   [4] p. 87.   [5] p. 76.

the exception of Lady Denham, they are not designed to support a leading role, while the lightly sketched trio, Charlotte, Clara, and Sidney, who promise to be the central figures, exert little control over the action, and invite no attachment of the readers' feelings. The threads of the plot compose no single, unifying pattern, and there are a number of lines of possible development: the fortunes of Sanditon and its backers; attempts on the wealth of Lady Denham; her plans for the marriage of Sir Edward and Esther; his plans for the seduction of Clara; the arrival of Sidney, to be followed by his friends, with the possibility of romance for Charlotte, Clara, and the Misses Beaufort. Is *Sanditon* to remain primarily a satire of modern idiosyncrasy, or is this element to be subordinated to an account of the heroine's deepening experience? These are some of the questions that I believe Jane Austen wished to provoke in order to create and sustain an air of uncertainty and dramatic suspense, which was to be pierced by a sudden shaft of enlightenment, a denouement which would probably involve the ballooning and comic collapse of all the various schemes and speculations.

If these uncertainties about the story are a sign that Jane Austen is changing her method, another such indication is a modification in her treatment of the fictional world. Until the concluding pages of her novels she handles the body of her stories as if they are literal, historical accounts, expanded and presented with the writer's privilege of selection, mobility, commentary, and insight. But in *Sanditon* the state of fictional illusion is deliberately and continually violated. Within the story the figures are granted an existence and verisimilitude of their own, yet they are constantly referred to as if they were literary types, creations filling roles in a burlesque or satire, just as we find Catherine Morland and Mrs. Allen treated at the opening of *Northanger Abbey*.[1] For the first eleven pages the Parkers are unnamed; they are simply a 'Gentleman' and a 'Lady',[2] until Mr. Parker is labelled as the 'Travellor'.[3] Mr. Heywood is introduced as 'the Proprietor of the Place';[4] Char-

[1] pp. 13–20.   [2] pp. 1 ff.   [3] pp. 5 ff.   [4] p. 4.

lotte is described as 'the visiting Young Lady';[1] chapter 3 opens
'Every Neighbourhood should have a great Lady—. The great
Lady of Sanditon, was Lady Denham';[2] when Mr. Parker tells
Charlotte about Clara she finds 'the interest of his story increased very much with the introduction of such a Character';[3]
and when she first sees that 'Interesting[4] young Woman'[5] her
impression is rendered largely in a parody description of the
conventional heroine:

> Elegantly tall, regularly handsome, with great delicacy of com-
> plexion & soft Blue eyes, a sweetly modest & yet naturally graceful
> Address, Charlotte could see in her only the most perfect representa-
> tion of whatever Heroine might be most beautiful & bewitching, in
> all the numerous vol:s they had left behind them on Mrs. Whitby's
> shelves ... she cd not separate the idea of a complete Heroine from
> Clara Brereton.[6]

This response is similar to that of Marianne Dashwood's first
sight of Willoughby: 'His person and air were equal to what
her fancy had ever drawn from the hero of a favourite story.'[7]

An even more extreme and self-conscious literary interpretation is given through Sir Edward Denham, who imagines himself to be 'quite in the line of the Lovelaces' and that 'To be
generally gallant & assiduous about the fair, to make fine
speeches to every pretty Girl, was but the inferior part of the
character he had to play'.[8] When Charlotte hears him describe
the sea she immediately places him as a familiar literary type,
Mackenzie's 'Man of Feeling'.[9] In the same way, when Mr.
Parker begins to expound his theories of sea-bathing and of the
commercial prospects of Sanditon, Jane Austen's family
audience would have recognized another of Mackenzie's characters, the Man of Spirit: 'In the various departments of business,

[1] p. 32.   [2] p. 31.   [3] p. 38.
[4] A word with heavy literary overtones from sentimental fiction; it usually
suggests that a person, or situation, is of 'sentimental' or romantic interest.
Jane Austen uses it with these associations in the novels, e.g. *Pride and Prejudice*, pp. 118, 150, 279; *Emma*, pp. 131, 181, 266, 335.
[5] p. 75.   [6] Ibid.   [7] *Sense and Sensibility*, p. 43.   [8] p. 110.
[9] p. 89. The archetype of this figure was Harley, *The Man of Feeling*
(1771) by Henry Mackenzie, whose work Jane Austen knew.

the term *spirit* is frequently applied to unprofitable projects and visionary speculations;'[1] and it is as a speculator and 'Projector' that Mr. Parker is seen by Charlotte.[2]

The illusion of a fictional reality is dispelled, or momentarily questioned, whenever Jane Austen labels the characters as literary figures, or when they look at one another in this way. In the case of Mr. Parker and Diana, the two eccentrics of whom we have the fullest picture, this duality, as realistic and created character, is further emphasized in their speech, for they have two manners, a special mode of delivery and jargon for their ruling passion, and a second manner and idiom for ordinary conversation. The movement between these two kinds of speech gives the effect of a character stepping in and out of his role. The Man of Spirit in Mr. Parker talks of Sanditon with the fluency of an estate-agent whose patter has been long preparing and often delivered. In this extract it is easy to follow the transition from his personal and familiar manner to the mounting eloquence of his sales-talk:

My name perhaps—tho' I am by no means the first of my Family, holding Landed Property in the Parish of Sanditon, may be unknown at this distance from the Coast—but Sanditon itself—everybody has heard of Sanditon,—the favourite—for a young & rising Bathing-place, certainly the favourite spot of all that are to be found along the coast of Sussex;—the most favoured by Nature, & promising to be the most chosen by Man.[3]

Sometimes the personal and professional manners of speech are merged; in moments of excitement or surprise his delivery becomes broken and staccato. Otherwise his personal style is loose and wordy, laced with tricks of phrase—*you know, I am sure, I fancy, I dare say*—a garrulity which emphasizes the ruminative quality of his thought.[4] The two contrasting elements in Diana's speech are of a more subtle variation. On one side we hear the personal note in her breathless and urgent enthusiasm as an organizer of other people's business:

Miss Lambe has an immense fortune—richer than all the rest—&

[1] *The Mirror*, no. 102.   [2] p. 130.   [3] p. 12.   [4] pp. 49–50.

very delicate health.—One sees clearly enough by all this, the *sort* of Woman Mrs. G. must be. . . . Here was a family of helpless Invalides whom I might essentially serve.—I sounded Susan—the same Thought had occurred to her.—Arthur made no difficulties—our plan was arranged immediately, we were off yesterday morng at 6—, left Chichester at the same hour today—& here we are.[1]

But closest to her heart, as Sanditon is to her brother's, is the sense of her own heroism in the face of ill-health, a topic that evokes a philosophical grandiloquence. As she moves into the second character, the colloquialisms and elliptical constructions give way to sentences carefully turned in the style of moral reflection:

But my dear Miss Heywood, we are sent into this World to be as extensively useful as possible, & where some degree of Strength of Mind is given, it is not a feeble body which will excuse us—or incline us to excuse ourselves.—The World is pretty much divided between the Weak of Mind & the Strong—between those who can act & those who can not, & it is the bounden Duty of the Capable to let no opportunity of being useful escape them.[2]

My belief that Jane Austen was moving into a new, experimental style, is strengthened by a study of passages of description and narrative where the writing is lively and varied to balance the emphatic speech-mannerisms of the eccentrics. Comparing the openings of *The Watsons*[3] and *Sanditon*[4] we find in the earlier piece the economy and clarity of detail, the concentration upon significant facts, so typical of Jane Austen's descriptive method. To serve this end the prose is usually brisk and neat, functioning unobtrusively. *Sanditon*, however, opens very differently. There is an elaboration of secondary detail not strictly relevant to the immediate action, and the focus of attention moves away from the event of the accident to the behaviour of the driver:

He had grumbled & shaken his shoulders so much indeed, and pitied & cut his Horses so sharply, that he might have been open to the suspicion of overturning them on purpose (especially as the Carriage was not his Masters own) if the road had not indisputably

[1] pp. 121–2.　　[2] pp. 123–4.　　[3] See above, pp. 66–67.　　[4] pp. 1–3.

become considerably worse than before, as soon as the premises of the said House were left behind—expressing with a most intelligent portentous countenance that beyond it no wheels but cart wheels could safely proceed.[1]

The awkwardness of this sentence is not, as one might expect, the clumsiness of an uncorrected trial, the difficulty of expression that an author may have to overcome before he warms to his story; nor is it due to a failure in the writer's critical censor. These lines are heavily corrected and revised. The roughness is a contrived effect, to enforce our sense of the driver's recalcitrance, the difficulty of the road, and the foundering of the coach. Never before had Jane Austen directed her style to such an end. Equally remarkable is the material being described, and its treatment. Our attention is drawn to details scarcely related to the accident or its consequences. The account of the driver's behaviour is prominent. We might well expect to meet him again, or to be shown a significant interplay of character and action. But he has no place in the story. His character is irrelevant to the action, although of course it may be relevant to some other aspect of the work, as yet unrevealed. Whatever intention we attribute to Jane Austen's design here, it is apparent that her technique and purpose of description and narration differ considerably from the method of the earlier novels.

There is a new element, too, in the description of objects and scenes. We are sufficiently aware of the countryside at Willingden, but no more so than is necessary for the placing of events, whereas Sanditon is presented with a fullness, a degree of reality not merely of observed features. More than anywhere else in Jane Austen's novels it possesses a unique spirit of place, an atmosphere of its own, unmistakably, for example, in the account of Charlotte's arrival, and in the description of the view from her window:

At Trafalgar House, rising at a little distance behind the Terrace, the Travellers were safely set down, & all was happiness & Joy between Papa & Mama & their Children; while Charlotte having

[1] pp. 1–2.

received possession of her apartment, found amusement enough in standing at her ample, Venetian window, & looking over the miscellaneous foreground of unfinished Buildings, waving Linen, & tops of Houses, to the Sea, dancing & sparkling in Sunshine and Freshness.[1]

There is energy in scene and action alike. This is the world for the optimism of Mr. Parker, and for the excitement of seaside speculation. The description and setting of Trafalgar House harmonize with the aspirations of its owner; the rhythm of this sentence is suitably nimble, its effect crisp and clear:

Trafalgar House, on the most elevated spot on the Down was a light elegant building, standing in a small Lawn with a very young plantation round it, about an hundred yards from the brow of a steep, but not very lofty Cliff—[1]

The description of the sea-front and village in the late afternoon is deepened, the scene is observed with sympathy and wit, an emotional penetration, as it were, of a breathing space in Sanditon's day:

here & there a solitary Elderly Man might be seen, who was forced to move early & walk for health—but in general, it was a thorough pause of Company, it was Emptiness & Tranquillity on the Terrace, the Cliffs, & the Sands.—The Shops were deserted—the Straw Hats & pendant Lace seemed left to their fate both within the House & without, and Mrs Whitby at the Library was sitting in her inner room, reading one of her own Novels, for want of Employment.[2]

And yet another effect is that of the 'misty morng'[3] on which Sidney comes into view and Charlotte (later) glimpses the two figures in the grounds of Sanditon House.

It is a feature of Jane Austen's art that the background of her stories, whether of country or town, should be appropriate to the mood or action. But only in the brief description of Lyme, and the account of Fanny's walk along the ramparts of Portsmouth, does she show a feeling for objects and scenes, convincing evidence that she was, as Henry Austen claims, 'a warm and judicious admirer of landscape, both in nature and on canvass'.[4] In the past she had kept landscape description to a

---

[1] pp. 55–56.   [2] pp. 69–70.
[3] p. 164.   [4] *Biographical Notice*, p. 7.

minimum, probably in reaction against the popular fashion of elaborate, set-piece scenery, such as we find in the novels of Mrs. Smith. Yet, as Mr. Forster remarks, in *Sanditon* 'topography comes to the front, and is screwed much deeper than usual into the story'.[1] This new interest may owe something to Burns, Scott, and Wordsworth. Crabbe, too, may have been a strong influence.[2] But it is important to notice Jane Austen's quite distinctive feeling for a social, populated landscape, with every-day man in a prosaic setting. Her close and witty observation is affectionate, almost tender.

Jane Austen's stylistic development can be followed in a third direction, in the use of reported speech, an *oratio obliqua* that retains the mannerisms of the living voice, which she had already used in *Emma*. This is employed extensively in presenting Mr. Parker, qualifying his enthusiasm with a touch of the creator's irony:

Sanditon was a second Wife & 4 Children to him—hardly less Dear—& certainly more engrossing.—He could talk of it for ever.— It had indeed the highest claims;—not only those of Birthplace, Property, and Home,—it was his Mine, his Lottery, his Speculation & his Hobby Horse; his Occupation his Hope & his Futurity.[3]

A more complex example illustrates the ease with which Jane Austen adjusts the tone of her reporting. Mr. Parker is recounting to Charlotte Lady Denham's experience on her visit to London:

She had gone to an Hotel—living by her own account as prudently as possible, to defy the reputed expensiveness of such a home, & at the end of three Days calling for her Bill, that she might judge of her state.—It's amount was such as determined her on staying not another hour in the House, & she was preparing in all the anger & perturbation which a beleif of very gross imposition *there*, & an ignorance of where to go for better usage, to leave the Hotel at all hazards, when the Cousins, the politic & lucky Cousins, who seemed always

---

[1] *Abinger Harvest*, p. 150.

[2] Jane Austen admired Crabbe (*Letters*, p. 370), and allusions in her correspondence reveal how well she and Cassandra knew *The Borough* (1810), (*Letters*, p. 358 n.), and *Tales* (1812), (*Letters*, p. 323 n.).

[3] p. 24.

to have a spy on her, introduced themselves at this important moment, & learning her situation, persuaded her to accept such a home for the rest of her stay as their humbler house in a very inferior part of London, cd. offer.[1]

The passage begins as a neutral account by Mr. Parker, representing Lady Denham's point of view, develops into a critical reading of the facts, a blend of commentary both by him and Jane Austen, and in the final lines conveys the polite humility of the cousins set off by Lady Denham's acid comment. Chapter 3, the context of this passage, is itself a large-scale example of Jane Austen's new technique in communicating information and varying the narrative point of view. Mr. Parker's account of Lady Denham contains details of her life far beyond what he could be expected to know. Jane Austen designs his account so that she can employ Charlotte's attentive, orderly mind to make sense of his observations, while at the same time keeping her own power to assume and resign control of the narrative without obvious intrusion. The chapter opens with an incisive aphorism and then moves easily into Mr. Parker's account, during which the author unobtrusively returns, and the complexity of the communication deepens. These techniques of representing speech, and of rendering speech within narrative, are constantly varied. Together with the qualities of description and narration they compose a suitably emphatic and diversified context for the eccentrics, whose credibility can only be maintained in a fictional world in which the other elements are drawn with equal strength.

(III)

The manuscript reveals nothing new about Jane Austen's process of writing, correction, and revision. She attends to the basic arts of story-telling, strengthening the time-sequences, the logic of cause and effect, the sentence structure, and the expressive power of her diction. As the general nature of these changes is similar to that illustrated in *The Watsons* and the two chapters of *Persuasion*, I shall confine my examination to

[1] pp. 39–40.

those alterations which indicate, or confirm, Jane Austen's intentions for the finished work. The extensive revision leaves the text in an advanced state, and I believe that it can be seen that we are dealing with a fragment that could take its place in the completed novel with little change.

Dr. Chapman attributes the roughness of the satire 'in part to lack of revision; she would have smoothed these coarse strokes, so strikingly different from the mellow pencillings of *Persuasion*.'[1] Dr. Chapman's guess may be right, but I have tried to suggest why the earlier novels are of small help in assisting us to theorize about the nature of the finished *Sanditon*; it is clearly a new departure. Further, the revisions show us that in so far as Jane Austen was changing the presentation of the characters, she was not toning down but heightening their traits and eccentricities. In this respect Mr. Parker receives most attention, largely to emphasize his speech mannerisms. The alterations range from the slightest adjustments of diction to larger changes, which stress fundamental aspects of his character. For instance, the vivid, colloquial nature of his expression is maintained: 'it would be a credit to the Place!' becomes, more emphatically, 'it would be a fine thing for the Place!'[2] 'I am very sorry to have brought you into this awkward Predicament' becomes 'I am very sorry to have brought you into this Scrape';[3] 'a great influx' becomes 'a prodigious influx'.[4] His fluency in recommending Sanditon is increased: the slightly clumsy expression, 'the most favoured by Nature, & consequently the most likely to be chosen by Man' becomes 'the most favoured by Nature, & promising to be the most chosen by Man'.[5] As a foil to his way of talking in short, sharp sentences, some of his expressions are bulked out with little catch-phrases,[6] and in revision this trick of speech is extended: *you know* is inserted in three places,[7] *in fact* once,[8] and on another occasion his manner

[1] *Facts and Problems*, p. 208.   [2] p. 50, note to l. 20.
[3] p. 10, note to l. 1.   [4] p. 22, note to l. 19.
[5] p. 12, note to l. 14.   [6] See above, p. 124.
[7] p. 10, note to l. 13; p. 35, note to l. 3; p. 44, note to l. 4.
[8] p. 45, note to l. 19.

is considerably formalized by this addition at the head of a sentence, 'Why, in truth Sir'.[1] There are other, more significant changes, relating to his character as an optimist, and to the theme of illusion and reality. Originally, when celebrating Sanditon's advantages, Mr. Parker glories that in its distance from London his village is 'a measured mile nearer than East Bourne. Only conceive Sir, the advantage of that in a long Journey.' This becomes, 'One complete, measured mile nearer than East Bourne. Only conceive Sir, the advantage of saving a whole Mile, in a long Journey.'[2] A similar example of emphatic repetition, an insistence on his own point of view, can be seen in the expressions of delight on discovering blue shoes in a Sanditon shopwindow. Into the body of his remarks two sentences are inserted: 'This is new within the Month. There was no blue Shoe when we passed this way a month ago.'[3] His obstinacy of belief is also deepened; in the face of Mr. Heywood's denials he maintains that there is a surgeon in the neighbourhood: 'Then Sir, I can bring proof of your having a Surgeon in the Parish'. Jane Austen reinforces this claim, adding to the sentence 'whether you may know it or not'.[4] In the same way his optimism is stressed. Old Stringer, whom Mr. Parker has set up as a market gardener, has not been successful; but, typically, Mr. Parker is sure 'He *will* do very well'. Jane Austen extends this expression, with the words 'beyond a doubt'.[5]

Similarly, the slight changes in Sir Edward's speech are usually to heighten his eccentricity, a literary affectation which inflates his diction: 'unconquerable' is replaced by the strange word 'indomptible',[6] 'sagacious' by 'anti-puerile',[7] 'what we have been doing' is formalized to 'what has been our Occupation',[8] 'his Rival' becomes 'any opposing Character'.[9] Likewise Lady Denham's vulgarisms are broadened: 'he needs it enough' becomes 'he needs it bad enough',[10] and 'We lived

---

[1] p. 17, note to l. 1.
[3] p. 53, note to l. 15.
[5] p. 49, note to l. 4.
[7] p. 108, note to l. 5.
[9] p. 107, note to l. 21.
[2] p. 15, notes to ll. 10, 13.
[4] p. 6, note to l. 20.
[6] p. 107, note to l. 10.
[8] p. 105, note to l. 8.
[10] p. 98, note to l. 4.

perfectly happily together' becomes 'Nobody could live happier together than us'.[1]

In the alterations affecting Charlotte the changes, like the increased emphasis on Mr. Parker's optimism and strength of opinion, are related generally to the theme of illusion and reality as well as to individual traits of character. The manuscript seems to confirm that her position in the fragment, and her probable place in the completed work, is that of the perceptive, observing heroine. When Charlotte meets Lady Denham and Clara for the first time Jane Austen inserts the sentence, 'She observed them well'.[2] Her perception is stressed again, during the conversation with Lady Denham, when she comments favourably on Sir Edward and 'directly saw that it was laying her open to suspicion'. This originally read, 'Charlotte imagined that it was laying her open to suspicion'.[3] At the end of this scene, when Charlotte is reflecting upon Lady Denham, Jane Austen's concern is to strengthen the comparison between the heroine and Mr. Parker. The original reading:

> She is much worse than I expected—meaner—a great deal meaner. She is very mean. Mr. Parker spoke too mildly of her. His own kind Disposition makes him judge too well of others . . .

becomes,

> She is thoroughly mean. I had not expected anything so bad.— Mr. P. spoke too mildly of her.—His Judgement is evidently not to be trusted.[4]

The passage continues in this vein; Charlotte's disapproval of Lady Denham is not removed, but transferred to a later position,[5] and the present topic is her analysis of the factors that prejudice Mr. Parker's view of his patron.

The other alterations that I want to call attention to are those which help to pin-point special features of style and technique. I have suggested that the structure and content of certain sentences give an effect that is entirely new to Jane Austen's

[1] p. 97, note to l. 4.
[2] p. 74, note to l. 11.
[3] p. 98, note to l. 18.
[4] p. 103, notes to ll. 12, 14.
[5] p. 104, ll. 1–3.

prose, and the revision shows this to be an effect worked for, not incidental to a first draft. In the description of the coach and driver already quoted[1] the alterations are heavy, but we can also see this new style conveniently illustrated in a passage only lightly revised.

A twinge or two, in trying to move his foot disposed the Travellor to think rather more as he had done at first of the benefit of immediate assistance—& consulting his wife in the few words of 'Well my Dear, I beleive it will be better for us.' (*originally* 'we had better accept this kind offer')—(*originally* he) turned again to Mr. H. . . .[2]

The sentence continues for another thirty-nine words, sustaining the thought, speech and action in its energetic development. The slight changes are to ease the rhythmical flow, and adjust the syntax to the scale of a long, loosely articulated period. Its bustling, sprightly movement catches Mr. Parker's manner of speech and action. Elsewhere, we can watch the process of revision investing a sentence with a surging, almost poetic rhythm. The original eulogy of Sanditon read,

It had indeed the highest claims;—Birthplace, Property, Home,—it was also his Mine, his Lottery, his Speculation & his Hobby Horse; his Hope & his Futurity.

This becomes:

It had indeed the highest claims;—not only those of Birthplace, Property, and Home,—it was his Mine, his Lottery, his Speculation & his Hobby Horse, his Occupation his Hope & his Futurity.[3]

The strong rhetorical note is developed not wholly in imitation of Mr. Parker's speech, but also to provide an attendant ironic reflection upon his claims and manner. Again, we can watch Jane Austen perfecting the brightness and vitality of the style, and pointing the wit of the ironic undertone in this commendation of the sea air and bathing. First Jane Austen wrote:

Nobody could catch cold by the Sea, Nobody wanted appetite by the Sea, nor cd the most obstinate Cougher retain a cough there

---

[1] See above, pp. 125–6.
[2] p. 11, notes to ll. 15, 16.   [3] p. 24, notes to ll. 7–10.

4 & 20 hours.—They were healing, softing, relaxing—fortifying & bracing—just as each was wanted—sometimes one, sometimes the other.

In revision these qualities are strengthened, in the first sentence by further parallelism of diction and structure, in the second by the slightest of changes, a neatening of the wit:

Nobody could catch cold by the Sea, Nobody wanted appetite by the Sea, Nobody wanted Spirits, Nobody wanted Strength.—They were healing, softing, relaxing—fortifying & bracing—seemingly just as was wanted—sometimes one, sometimes the other.[1]

Another characteristic of the style is the limited but striking use of figurative language, which can be isolated in certain manuscript alterations. For example, there is a series of three changes in this description of Sanditon, developing a tension between the abstract phrase and the delicate personification: first 'a something of note' becomes 'a something of young notoriety' and then, as a final version, 'a something of young Renown'.[2] Other changes extend the idiomatic flavour of Diana Parker's speech: 'I know where to apply' becomes 'I could soon put the necessary Irons in the fire.'[3] Believing that she has assisted Mrs. Griffiths in her plans to visit Sanditon, 'she was now regaling in the delight of opening the first Trenches of an acquaintance with such a powerful discharge of unexpected Obligation.'[4]

I have confined my attention to those alterations on the manuscript that draw attention to the theme, the liveliness of the writing, the vividness of character portrayal, some aspects of the fragment which prompt us to regard it as the beginning to a highly original work. One marvels that a sick woman, an experienced novelist now confirmed in her methods and style, should make a departure of this kind so late in life. Perhaps it was the writer's demon, the compulsive force of inspiration which will have its own way—putting out of view all behests but its own, dictating certain words, and insisting on their being used,

[1] p. 25, notes to ll. 17, 19.   [2] p. 21, note to l. 6.
[3] p. 62, note to l. 11.   [4] p. 135, note to l. 5.

whether vehement or measured in their nature; new moulding characters, giving unthought of turns to incidents, rejecting carefully elaborated old ideas, and suddenly creating and adopting new ones.[1]

Was *Sanditon* the product of an imagination stimulated in ill health? Or can it be regarded as the creator's protest against her condition, the artist's lively and energetic compensation for the state of the body? The account of Jane Austen's illness that we can piece together from the family records implies that she was suffering a malignant internal condition, which brought on periods of debility varied with other times of renewed strength, such that a few days before her death, when she composed and wrote out the poem 'Venta',[2] some weeks after *Sanditon* had been abandoned out of physical exhaustion. Although such causal explanations are irrelevant in matters of critical judgement, the questions are perplexing, to be entertained, if not to be answered. The modern reader may also wonder how fully the imaginative life of this work was to reveal Jane Austen's response to the forces of the Romantic movement. But the fragment ends too soon, and the answer to this question, like many others, is beyond recovery. All that remains is the evidence of the writer's creative sensibility, the continuing power of her imagination to respond to fresh experience and form it anew. 'Catching the very note and trick, the strange irregular rhythm of life, that is the attempt whose strenuous force keeps Fiction upon her feet.'[3] Henry James was describing his own sense of the novelist's task. His words might well stand as an epigraph to *Sanditon*, the work in which Jane Austen strove as never before to catch 'the very note and trick, the strange irregular rhythm' in the new life of the nineteenth century.

[1] Charlotte Brontë in a letter to G. H. Lewes, 12 January 1848 (see above, p. 100).

[2] It has been supposed that the author of this poem was her brother James, but I am convinced that the attribution to Jane is correct. For a full discussion of this point see my note, 'Jane Austen', *The Times Literary Supplement*, 30 November 1962, p. 944.

[3] 'The Art of Fiction' (1884), in *The House of Fiction* (1957), ed. Leon Edel, p. 38.

APPENDIX

Theories of Composition for Mansfield Park and Emma[1]

At a number of points in this study I have found myself in disagreement with the views argued by Mrs. Leavis in 'A Critical Theory of Jane Austen's Writings',[2] an extensive and detailed examination of Jane Austen's method of composition. Mrs. Leavis claims that in the writing of the novels Jane Austen drew widely upon the events of her own life, on the lives of those around her, on her reading, and on the juvenilia and early pieces. She asserts that this process of creation can be *shown* to have taken place, and insists that unless we examine Jane Austen's procedure in composition 'no criticism of her novels can be just or even safe.'[3] This proposition is supported by a detailed analysis. Mrs. Leavis offers to show, firstly, how *Mansfield Park* was written out of *Lady Susan*, which, in turn, had been based upon the author's observation of the courtship of Henry Austen and Eliza de Feuillide; and secondly, how *Emma* was written out of *The Watsons*. Some years ago, in *Facts and Problems*,[4] Dr .Chapman indicated a number of objections to be entered against the *Theory*, but as it has remained otherwise unchallenged[5] and its findings generally accepted,[6] I feel obliged to set out the grounds of my disagreement concerning the two manuscript works, *Lady Susan* and *The Watsons*.

Before discussing particular points in the *Theory* I want to consider briefly the kind and degree of relationship that we can discern between Jane Austen's novels and her life. Confusion about this matter dates

---

[1] Certain passages in this Appendix are taken from 'Mrs. Leavis and Miss Austen: the "Critical Theory" Reconsidered', © 1962 by The Regents of the University of California, by whose permission they are reprinted from *Nineteenth-century Fiction*, xvii. 21–32.

[2] *Scrutiny*, x (1941), 61–90, 114–42, (1942) 272–94; xii (1944), 104–19.

[3] Ibid., x. 86.   [4] Ch. 8, 'Fact and Fiction'.

[5] Marvin Mudrick, *Jane Austen: Irony as Defense and Discovery* (1952), pp. 260–3, disagrees with one or two of Mrs. Leavis's points, although he appears to accept the *Theory* as a whole. Robert Liddell, *The Novels of Jane Austen* (1963), similarly questions or qualifies particular details in the *Theory*, but works within its premises.

[6] Most recently, for example, in *The Literary Critics* (1962) by George Watson, where it is described as 'a careful and brilliant group of articles' (p. 212), and by Graham Hough in *The Listener* (7 November 1963, p. 749).

from the publication of *Sense and Sensibility*. Jane Austen was immediately troubled with readers who imagined that they could identify originals for her characters—Marianne and Elinor were read as portraits of the author and her sister. *Pride and Prejudice* was read in the same way. Sir Walter Scott tells of a friend 'whom the author never saw or heard of . . . at once recognised by his own family as the original of Mr. Bennet'.[1] A month after the publication of *Mansfield Park* Jane Austen met a Miss Dusautoy who had 'a great idea of being Fanny Price—she and her youngest sister together, who is named Fanny'.[2] After the appearance of *Emma* she noted that a Miss Herries was 'convinced that I had meant Mrs & Miss Bates for some acquaintance of theirs—People whom I never heard of before.—'[3] These and other identifications are naïve tributes to the force of her character-drawing.

But Jane Austen was not flattered by this confusion between art and life. She repudiated the suggestion that her figures were modelled upon friends, and denied that their oddities had been recorded. She is reported to have expressed 'a dread of what she called such an "invasion of the social proprieties" '.[4] The reminiscences of Caroline Austen confirm this point. She writes of her aunt's 'kindly restraint' and 'regard' for her neighbours:

> She liked immensely to hear all about them. They sometimes served for her amusement, but it was her own nonsense that gave zest to the gossip—She never turned *them* into ridicule—She was as far as possible from being either censorious or satirical—she never abused them or *quizzed* them—[5]

Jane Austen emphasized that 'it was her desire to create, not to reproduce',[6] a point made with equal force in the *Biographical Notice*, where Henry wrote that 'Her power of inventing characters seems to have been intuitive, and almost unlimited. She drew from nature; but, whatever may have been surmised to the contrary, never from individuals.'[7] He would have known well enough that surmises had been made to the contrary, and he felt obliged to address those readers who were unable to understand his sister's art. Perhaps he could remember how years before, in 1798, the Steventon household

[1] Mentioned in the *Quarterly Review* notice of *Emma*, p. 194.
[2] *Letters*, p. 391.
[3] 'Opinions of *Emma*' in *Plan of a Novel*, p. 21.
[4] 1870 *Memoir*, p. 202.
[5] *My Aunt*, p. 8.
[6] 1870 *Memoir*, p. 203.   [7] pp. 7–8.

had laughed over Egerton Brydges' latest novel, *Arthur Fitz-Albini*, and how they had tried to recognize the characters, amongst whom they thought they saw at least three of their acquaintances. Jane Austen was herself contemptuous of the book, largely because it offended her sense of literary and social decorum: 'Never did any book carry more internal evidence of its author. Every sentiment is completely Egerton's.'[1]

With her strict view of the author's privacy and anonymity so clearly and emphatically stated, there is no reason to doubt James Edward Austen-Leigh's assertion that Jane Austen's own relations 'never recognized any individuals in her characters'.[2] When it was suggested to Francis Austen that he might be the original for Captain Harville he rejected the not unflattering identification, consenting only to the possibility of portrayal in minor detail: 'I rather think parts of Captain Harville's character were drawn from myself; at least the description of his domestic habits, tastes and occupations have a considerable resemblance to mine.'[3] Francis was visiting Chawton Cottage almost daily in October and November 1815 when Jane had just started work on *Persuasion*, and it is more than likely that she observed his manners and conversation. She may also have consulted him then over naval matters, just as she had a few years before in the writing of *Mansfield Park*,[4] for which she borrowed the names of three of his ships. The amber cross which William Price brought to his sister from Sicily may be Jane Austen's grateful reminder of the 'gold chains & Topaze crosses'[5] that Charles Austen had sent his sisters from the Mediterranean in 1801. This would be wholly consistent with her dependence upon the real world for the basis of fictional creation.[6]

While recognizing, then, that there is, at certain points, a direct relationship between Jane Austen's life and her art, we must beware of attributing undue significance to similarities between the novels and the real world. Jane Austen's plots, characters, and settings are the familiar surroundings of her own social group. The novels, and much of her other writing, present the experiences of young women as they move through love to marriage. Among the six novels,

---

[1] Letter to Cassandra, 25 November 1798 (*Letters*, p. 32).
[2] 1870 *Memoir*, p. 202.
[3] Quoted by J. H. Hubback, 'Pen Portraits in Jane Austen's Novels', *Cornhill Magazine*, lxv (1928), 25.
[4] *Letters*, pp. 317, 340.   [5] Ibid., p. 137.
[6] For further examples see *Letters*, note to p. 292, and p. 412.

a quantity of smaller works, and over five hundred pages of letters resemblances among figures, settings, and incidents are inevitable. That likenesses occur is a matter of course, not an invitation to speculate. Mrs. Leavis finds that Jane Austen's letters are full of character sketches which 'often appear in a recognizable form in the novels'.[1] She cites Mr. Lushington from Letter 87, a figure who 'suggests Mr. Walter Elliott, or Harriet Moore's husband who suggests Mr. John Knightley, or Miss Milles and her mother who suggest Miss Bates and hers—the list is endless'.[2] Yes, the list is indeed endless, not because Jane Austen took her characters directly from life (and it is Mrs. Leavis's theory that this is demonstrably so) but because they are so lifelike. Tributes to the realism of her character-drawing are a staple of contemporary reviews and early criticism. Due weight should be given to Scott's praise of *Emma* in the *Quarterly Review* (op. cit.) and to the comment of another contemporary novelist, Susan Ferrier, who remarked (again, of *Emma*) that the 'characters are all so true to life'.[3] Reproduction or imitation are no part of her aim; whereas verisimilitude and fidelity to common experience are inseparable from her concept of artistic truth.

Much of the speculation about Jane Austen's supposed originals has been unpretentious. In A. C. Bradley's fine essay[4] there is a passing reference to the likeness between Miss Bates and Miss Milles, an observation that was taken up by Katharine Metcalf, the editor of the Oxford *Pride and Prejudice* (1912), who further suggested that the portrait of Lady Catherine de Bourgh might be based upon Mary Lloyd, James's second wife.[5] But when in 1920 Mary Augusta Austen-Leigh declared *Lady Susan* to be a 'Study from Life',[6] the search for originals was to become a major distraction in Jane Austen studies.

Although Miss Austen-Leigh enjoyed access to family papers (through her father, the author of the 1870 *Memoir*), little reliance can be placed upon her account of the origin of *Lady Susan*. She gives the story of Mrs. Craven,[7] a cruel society woman who so maltreated her daughters that they ran away from home. One of them, Martha Craven, became the wife of the Rev. Nowys Lloyd

---

[1] *Scrutiny*, xii. 118.   [2] Ibid.
[3] *Memoir and Correspondence of Susan Ferrier* (1898), ed. J. A. Doyle, undated letter (1816) to Miss Clavering, p. 128.
[4] 'Jane Austen', *Essays and Studies*, ii (1911), 7–36.
[5] p. 403.   [6] *Personal Aspects*, p. 104.
[7] Unnamed by Miss Austen-Leigh, but identified by Dr. Chapman, *Facts and Problems*, p. 52.

in 1763, whose daughters, Eliza, Martha, and Mary, were lifelong friends of Jane Austen. From them she could have heard the story of their mother's persecution and escape. But the theory that Mrs. Craven is the prototype for Lady Susan depends entirely upon two circumstantial points: firstly, correspondence in detail; secondly, the nature of *Lady Susan* as the work of a young woman, supposing Jane Austen to have been about twenty at the time of composition. The parallels between the history of Mrs. Craven and Jane Austen's story are trivial, being no more than similarities of situation. The persecuted daughter and the tyrannical mother are as common in literature as in life; it is a stock situation in the distresses of the sentimental heroine. Miss Austen-Leigh's second line of argument stems from her surprise that a young girl could produce 'this remarkable analysis of a vicious woman's nature',[1] and she concludes: 'without having constantly before her thoughts the prototype of this exceptional character' Jane Austen would have been unable to depict 'an inhuman, repulsive mother'.[2] This assumption reveals a complete misunderstanding of the writer's creative imagination.[3] It is a point of view that probably derives from the *Life*, whose authors were equally surprised 'that an inexperienced girl should have had independence and boldness enough to draw at full length a woman of the type of Lady Susan'.[4] Miss Austen-Leigh's argument looks very much like a case of special pleading. In common with other family biographers she feels obliged to explain away *Lady Susan*, under the misapprehension that it would be a slur on Jane Austen's character and literary reputation to suppose this adulterous, unprincipled heroine to have been as fully a product of her imagination as the mature novels.

Later critics have ignored the Lady Susan–Mrs. Craven equation, offering in its place another series of identifications, successively more complicated and conjectural. In 1928 Mr. J. H. Hubback (a grandson of Francis Austen) wrote: 'I have come to the conclusion, probably not altogether an original one, that the character of Mary Crawford may be founded, to some extent, on that of Jane's cousin and sister-in-law, Eliza'.[5] In 1890 Goldwin Smith had noted that the character of Lady Susan 'uniting charms with vices may be

---

[1] *Personal Aspects*, p. 100.   [2] Ibid., p. 103.
[3] Compare Mrs. Leavis, Introduction to *Sense and Sensibility* (1958), p. xix: Lady Susan, 'a beautiful and well-bred Becky Sharp could hardly have been invented by young Miss Austen'.   [4] p. 81.
[5] Op. cit., above, p. 138.

regarded as a rude and coarse germ of that of Mary Crawford'.[1] The next step, duly taken by Miss C. L. Thomson in 1929 was to connect Eliza with Lady Susan.[2] The equation is completed by Mrs. Leavis. The various ideas are welded together into a continuous argument—the proposition that Eliza de Feuillide is the original of Lady Susan, that Lady Susan/Eliza becomes Mary Crawford, and that *Lady Susan* provides the basis for *Mansfield Park*.

The core of this argument is that *Lady Susan* tells of the courtship of Henry Austen and Eliza; that Henry (with the addition of traits derived from Edgar Mandlebert in *Camilla*) is the model for Reginald, as Eliza is for Lady Susan, and that Jane Austen holds the position of Mrs. Vernon, the disapproving sister who observes these events. In point of fact there is an amazing real-life resemblance between Eliza and Lady Susan. Thirty-two of Eliza's letters to her cousin Philadelphia Walter have survived, dating between May 1780, when she was eighteen, and October 1801.[3] They catch the very tone and style of Lady Susan's letters to Mrs. Johnson. Eliza reveals herself (as she is also described in Philadelphia's six letters to her brother James) as an almost exact image of Jane Austen's heroine—witty, shrewd, calculating, flirtatious, jealous of her reputation, yet unable to preserve herself from scandal, a heartless mother, domineering with men, and glorying in their adoration, but essentially shallow in her feelings. Her interest in Henry dates from her arrival at Steventon in 1787, where she took a leading part in the theatricals. Seven years later the Comte de Feuillide was executed in Paris. She was able to enjoy what she called the 'dear Liberty'[4] of widowhood, the freedom to look round for a second advantageous marriage. After considering the financial and social prospects of several matches she eventually married Henry in December 1797, having first overcome his wish to enter the Church (which he did in 1816, three years after her death). Her letters tell a fascinating story, remarkably similar to the career of Lady Susan; indeed, many passages might well be mistaken for Jane Austen's own work. Here, for example, is Eliza's answer to an inquiry by Philadelphia about herself and Henry (in July 1797):

For my own part I think this young man ill-used but the lady is so well pleased with her present situation that she cannot find in her

[1] *Life of Jane Austen*, p. 182.
[2] *Jane Austen: a Survey*; a considerable proportion of this work is devoted to establishing connexions between the life and writings.
[3] *Austen Papers*, chs. iv, v, vi.   [4] Ibid., p. 156.

heart to change it, and says in her giddy way that independence and
the homage of half a dozen are preferable to subjection and the attachment of a single individual. I am more & more convinced that she is
not at all calculated for sober matrimony. . . .[1]

In February 1798, only six weeks after their marriage, she wrote
to Philadelphia, describing life at the militia camp where Henry
was Adjutant: 'there are some with whom I think you would not
dislike a flirtation. I have *of course entirely* left off *trade*.'[2] Whatever
Eliza meant by this last remark, the implications of its heavy irony are
distasteful, and they are exactly in the character of Lady Susan.

Had the *Austen Papers* been available to Mrs. Leavis, her claim to
identification could have been stronger still. For example, because
she was unaware of Eliza's lack of affection for the child of her first
marriage, Mrs. Leavis was forced to suppose that Lady Susan's
heartlessness towards Frederica was a trait derived from Mrs. Craven
(an assumption that enables Mrs. Leavis to avoid contradicting
Miss Austen-Leigh). Yet this remarkable similarity between Eliza
and Lady Susan is similarity, and nothing more. Paradoxically, these
startling likenesses serve only to warn us how dangerous it is to argue
a claim of significant relationship on grounds of resemblance. For the
weight of evidence—textual, literary, and historical—makes it impossible to accept that Lady Susan is a portrait of Eliza, or that any
part of the work can be an account of Henry's courtship.

In the first place the internal evidence indicates that *Lady Susan*
was already written by 1795, before these family events had taken
place. By the style, subject-matter, and treatment, we are able to judge
that *Lady Susan* was composed immediately after the last of the juvenilia, late in 1793 or 1794.[3] In November 1797 Jane Austen began
to rewrite the epistolary *Elinor and Marianne* as the direct narrative
Sense and Sensibility. Mrs. Leavis takes it for granted that *Lady
Susan* was composed later than 1797, and on the authority of this
dating we are to suppose that Jane Austen reverted to the letter
form which experiments over the previous years had led her to
discard.

Further, the style of *Lady Susan* does not encourage one to suppose that a contingent family drama had been turned into art. Surely,
in those circumstances, Jane Austen's emotional warmth—her
anxious love for Henry, her distaste for Eliza—would be com-

---

[1] *Austen Papers*, p. 162.   [2] Ibid., p. 170.
[3] See above, pp. 46–47.

municated to the work, not necessarily in a direct and obvious manner, but perhaps in some special quality, an intensity, a sense of emotion repressed or controlled. But there is no such quality in *Lady Susan*, no warmth of feeling, no asperity towards the villainess, no sympathy for Reginald (who is something of a prig), no sense that the action has been observed,[1] or the emotions experienced. The mode of presentation, the style and tone, give the work a slightly frozen air, an effect of detachment, a distinct contrast to the impression we receive from the juvenilia pieces, 'Letter the third' and 'Letter the fourth', whose quality does tempt one to suppose them written out of personal experience.

The subsequent history of the manuscript, and its publication, settle the force of the argument directly against the possibility of a biographical interpretation. Everything we know about the Austen family points to their loyalty, and their jealous concern for Jane Austen's reputation. Are we to suppose that Cassandra, who took possession of her sister's literary effects in 1817, would allow such a damaging account of Henry's intimate affairs to remain in existence?[2] Would Henry permit such a portrait of his wife to pass round the family? We know that the manuscript circulated amongst them, and at least one copy was made during his lifetime. J. E. Austen-Leigh was keenly alive to the propriety of allowing his aunt's minor pieces into print. If the least hint of private scandal had attached to *Lady Susan* it is inconceivable that he would have taken the responsibility for making public such an episode of the family history. Even if those most deeply involved in these events were blind, or shut their eyes to the source of *Lady Susan*, what prevented the authors of the *Memoir* and *Life*, knowing *Lady Susan* and the documents printed

[1] We are not even certain that Jane Austen could have witnessed the courtship. Unfortunately, the records of this period are very scanty, but Henry was not staying at Steventon continuously between 1796–8, neither was Eliza a constant visitor, and in Jane Austen's seven letters (9 January 1796 to 18 September 1796; none survive from 1797, and the next is 8 April 1798) there is no suggestion that Henry's personal affairs were causing any concern to the family.

[2] In almost every one of the family biographies and memoirs there is reference to Cassandra's zealous destruction of any of her sister's letters which she considered too private for posterity: e.g. *Personal Aspects*: 'the great mass of Jane's letters were destroyed by Cassandra . . . she kept *only* those which she considered so totally devoid of general interest that it was impossible anyone should, at any time, contemplate their publication' (p. 48). In these circumstances it is unlikely that she would allow family history, in the shape of *Lady Susan*, to pass among later generations.

in the *Austen Papers*, from coming to the same conclusion as Mrs. Leavis? It is ingenuity, not insight, which sustains the *Theory* at this point.

The argument that *Mansfield Park* was written out of *Lady Susan* is equally implausible. It assumes the existence of an intervening epistolary version of *Mansfield Park*, written about 1808–9. Mrs. Leavis discerns in this novel what she calls a 'dimmed and distant effect'[1] pointing, it is said, to a letter origin. On the other hand, we are able to see quite clearly in the juvenilia letters that this form in no way curtails her liveliness of style and dramatic presentation. It is a narrative method which does not prevent direct conversation, nor need it limit the description of scenes and situations. Moreover, according to Mrs. Leavis, *Pride and Prejudice* was also originally cast in letters,[2] and that, of all the novels, is the one to which the terms 'dimmed and distant' would least apply. Thus, even if for the sake of argument we allow that *Mansfield Park* is distinguished by such an effect, it does not follow that we accept, as a consequence, a letter origin for the work. The theory of the epistolary ur-*Mansfield Park* encounters two more objections. Firstly, it is even more unreasonable than with *Lady Susan* to suppose that Jane Austen should have returned to the letter form at this time in her career, when she had firmly turned her back upon it at least ten years before. Secondly, the *Theory* (here, and elsewhere) throws doubt upon Cassandra's memorandum, which gives no hint of such a version. As I have suggested,[3] there is every reason to trust the accuracy and authority of that note.

The transformation of *Lady Susan* into *Mansfield Park* demands lengthy explanation, and I am compelled to summarize Mrs. Leavis's argument. The claim that *Lady Susan* is drawn from life involves a simple equation between the three pairs of fictional–real characters. The change of *Lady Susan* is much more complicated, for the story has to provide for a larger cast. Mrs. Leavis demonstrates the economy of Jane Austen's invention: Lady Susan is split up into two characters, Mary and Henry Crawford (this reveals the source of the 'personal animus manifested against Mary Crawford',[4] for she is really Eliza 'altered almost out of recognition').[5] The Bertram

[1] x. 115.
[2] I suggest this possibility on entirely different grounds, see above, pp. 53–54.
[3] See above, pp. 58–59, 62.   [4] *Scrutiny*, x. 115.
[5] Ibid., p. 133.

sisters come from 'Lesley Castle', the early work to which the
author turned when she 'was looking for more characters to fill out
the new story'.[1] Mrs. Norris is a re-working of Lady Greville in
'Letter the third', which also provided Maria Williams. Maria
Williams, joined with Frederica and Mrs. Vernon, becomes Fanny
Price. Lady Bertram is a composite figure, derived partly from
Mrs. Allen in *Northanger Abbey*, and partly from Lady Elmwood in
Mrs. Inchbald's *A Simple Story* (1791). Mrs. Johnson is divided into
three characters—Mr. Harding, Lady Stornaway, and Mrs. Fraser;
and Mr. Johnson becomes Mr. Fraser. Among other transformations
are Sir James Martin into Mr. Rushworth, Sir Reginald de Courcy
into Sir Thomas Bertram and Reginald into Edmund.

There comes a time when one has to put down the *Theory* in
bewilderment—where is it to end? So freely does Mrs. Leavis
assume the transposition of characters (which can be 'altered almost
out of recognition')—from life, from earlier pieces, and from other
authors—that the task of tracing Jane Austen's sources becomes
endless and meaningless. In pursuit of evidence Mrs. Leavis loses
all sense of what must be the criteria of relevance in this matter.
We are left with the impression that any of the characters in *Mansfield Park* might be evolved from an infinite number of prototypes.
The last word can be left to Dr. Chapman. In a letter to the *Times
Literary Supplement*, regarding Mrs. Leavis's contentions for *Mansfield Park*, he rejected 'the theory identifying Mary Crawford with
Jane Austen's sister-in-law Eliza, which Mrs Leavis seems to accept
as basic', and declared himself 'unable to accept many of her conclusions, which seemed to me to pass the limits of legitimate reconstruction'.[2]

Mrs. Leavis's other large-scale demonstration is of the change of
The Watsons into *Emma*. At first sight this may not appear to be such
a far-fetched theory. It has been presented by a number of critics,
and even finds some support from Dr. Chapman. In 1913 Warre
Cornish remarked upon the parallels between the two works;[3] Miss
Thomson extended the comparison and claimed a source relationship
between the stories ('such identifications are amusing and interesting');[4] and in the following year, 1930, Brimley Johnson wrote at
some length in favour of such connexion.[5] Finally, in *Facts and Problems*, Dr. Chapman gave his opinion that '*The Watsons* may with some
plausibility be regarded as a sketch for *Emma*.'[6]

[1] Ibid., 135.   [2] 18 December 1948, p. 713.   [3] *Jane Austen*, p. 226.
[4] Op. cit., p. 176.   [5] *Jane Austen*, pp. 79–86.   [6] p. 51.

In broadest outline there are these resemblances: the name Emma is common to both heroines; the action takes place in Surrey; there is a ball in which someone is rescued from acute embarrassment by an invitation to dance; and the heroines' fathers are self-centred invalids. Dr. Chapman finds 'Mrs. Robert Watson is strikingly suggestive of Mrs. Elton. Emma Watson is very like Jane Fairfax in situation, and—so far as we get to know her—not unlike Emma Woodhouse in character.'[1] Some of these relationships appear in Mrs. Leavis's argument, which I shall not examine in detail, since the character transformations are, for the most part, of the same order as those proposed for the *Lady Susan–Mansfield Park* change, and are thus open to the objections I have already raised. I do, however, wish to consider the prime connexion, that which has been claimed between Emma Watson and Emma Woodhouse. It is the central point of Mrs. Leavis's *Theory*, as it is of the earlier critics. Yet what is really outstanding in the characters and situations of the two girls is not likeness but contrast. To insist upon the many differences between the two heroines may seem to be stressing the obvious, but some objection to this part of the *Theory* seems to be especially required in view of the support it finds among other critics.

The fundamental difference is one of vision and personality. Emma Watson is witty, self-assured, and perceptive. She knows herself, and is quick to judge others, fairly and correctly, but for the slightest touch of primness. She is a mature woman, with moral sense, rational powers, seriousness, and tolerance far beyond her years. Although Emma Woodhouse is a year older, she is, by comparison, a mere child—self-conceited, self-indulgent, high-spirited, fanciful, and without any inclination towards the seriousness of mind and temper displayed by Emma Watson. The earlier heroine is a study in sober perfection, with a single fault, perhaps, in her scrupulous delicacy. The later heroine is a lively girl, at times wilful and foolish, who has to learn slowly by her mistakes. To ignore these essential points of contrast is to neglect a central concern in Jane Austen's art—the discrimination amongst characters who are superficially alike, the observation of difference in likeness, the fine gradations which distinguish one fool, bore, or marriageable young woman from the next. And in this case it is not a matter of fine gradations but of broad contrasts. Whereas Emma Woodhouse is a rich and pampered child,

---

[1] *Facts and Problems*, p. 51.

spoilt by her father and governess, and deferred to by the entire neighbourhood, Emma Watson is a Cinderella figure, a scarcely regarded daughter, the youngest girl in a large and impoverished family, herself having just lost any prospects of fortune, and now returned to Stanton a social nonentity. Mrs. Leavis has no difficulty in accounting for these unmistakable points of difference; by her account, this is merely resemblance-in-reverse.

Jane Austen abandoned *The Watsons* after having written about 17,500 words. Mrs. Leavis is happy to accept the guess (it is no more than that) of J. E. Austen-Leigh that Jane Austen left the work when she 'became aware of the evil of having placed her heroine too low, in such a position of poverty and obscurity', a situation that has a tendency to degenerate into 'vulgarity'.[1] Accepting this explanation, and proceeding further, Mrs. Leavis claims that in writing *Emma* Jane Austen returned to the fragment, 'to make a fresh start with the same materials by shaking the kaleidoscope to make a new pattern. . . . A new Emma was required who should be free from the "low" circumstances in her immediate person, so Emma Woodhouse becomes a real heiress; she is a more pronounced character—frank and decisive—to suit her altered circumstances.'[2] As I have said earlier,[3] Austen-Leigh's guess at Jane Austen's reason for abandoning the story is palpably mistaken. There are equally 'low' circumstances in *Mansfield Park*; and the direction of the plot was to save Emma from her so-called 'vulgarity' of situation. Jane Austen's dissatisfaction with the work was on very different grounds.

Mrs. Leavis accounts for the remarkable transformation of the heroine, and the change of the setting, as the shake of the 'kaleidoscope'. One resemblance that Mrs. Leavis considers of major importance is that of the ball scenes. The superficial similarities are obvious enough. But could it not be that the shaking of the 'kaleidoscope' resulted, not in the dance at the Crown in *Emma*, but in that at Netherfield, in *Pride and Prejudice*? The parallels are far closer. There are many resemblances in this scene: of Elizabeth to Emma Watson, of Darcy to Lord Osborne, of Bingley to Tom Musgrave, and further similarities in the action and dialogue. Nor need we stop at the ball. The basic situation of *The Watsons* is far closer to *Pride and Prejudice* than to *Emma*. Emma Watson, like Elizabeth Bennet, is a heroine of superior abilities and fine nature in a household whose

[1] 1871 *Memoir*, p. 296.
[2] *Scrutiny*, x. 37.　　　　　　　　　　　[3] See above, pp. 64–65.

members are intent on marriage, and where the father exerts little control. And during Lord Osborne's visit to Stanton we can watch, in miniature, an aspect of the general change in Darcy's manner towards Elizabeth. This is not to say that I suspect parts of *Pride and Prejudice* to have been derived from *The Watsons*, or vice versa. It is enough to illustrate that Mrs. Leavis's method of tracing sources can be applied with equal effect to indicate the possibility of influence in a number of directions, some of them equally impressive but wholly inconsistent. It is, of course, possible that *Emma* may actually have been written out of *The Watsons*; but unless we discover stronger evidence of the change, this unlikely process of creation, as with the suggested transformation of *Lady Susan* into *Mansfield Park*, cannot be shown to have taken place.

INDEX

INDEX

PRINTED IN GREAT BRITAIN
AT THE UNIVERSITY PRESS, OXFORD
BY VIVIAN RIDLER
PRINTER TO THE UNIVERSITY